TIME *for a* CHANGE

—— *Ideal Leadership Series* ——

Larry W. Stout, Ph.D.

DESTINY IMAGE® PUBLISHERS, INC.
P.O. Box 310, Shippensburg, PA 17257-0310

"Speaking to the Purposes of God for this
Generation and for the Generations to Come."

This book and all other Destiny Image, Revival Press, Mercy Place, Fresh Bread, Destiny Image Fiction, and Treasure House books are available at Christian bookstores and distributors worldwide.

For a U.S. bookstore nearest you, call 1-800-722-6774.
For more information on foreign distributors, call 717-532-3040.
Or reach us on the Internet: www.destinyimage.com

ISBN 10: 0-7684-2384-8
ISBN 13: 978-0-7684-2384-6

For Worldwide Distribution, Printed in the U.S.A.
1 2 3 4 5 6 7 8 9 10 11 / 09 08 07 06

Endorsements

Larry has provided me with high quality, professional, and emotionally intelligent advice on managerial and leadership challenges that I myself have been facing as a newly appointed manager. The concept of an ideal leadership model is not just a theoretical construction; it is a living creature. I know it.

Dina Grube, Director
World Bank Latvia

Larry Stout has the rare gift of taking complex subjects and making them simple to understand. His teachings have had a great impact on the new generation of managers in the Baltic countries.

Dr. Anders Paalzow, Rector
Stockholm School of Economics in Riga

Professor Larry Stout's extensive experience in mentoring and coaching people of different cultures and backgrounds qualifies him more than others to reflect and research on what "ideal" leadership is about.

Professor Andreas Kelling
Institute of Business Research
Neustadt, Germany

Compelling thoughts...challenging analysis. For the past 15 years anxious anticipation describes my reaction to any new writings by Larry Stout. I recommend Larry to you. You will not escape untouched when you read his writings.

Bob Snyder M.D., President
International Health Services

Dedication

To my dear wife, Debbie, whose persistence and love has kept my shoulder to the wheel, my nose to the grindstone, my eye on the ball, my ear to the ground—and what was left of me on the computer.

Table of Contents

Foreword 9

PART ONE: WHAT IS LEADERSHIP?

CHAPTER ONE

Understanding the Mystery—
Why Leadership Doesn't Make Sense 17

CHAPTER TWO

Unraveling the Mystery—
The Ideal Leadership Model 37

PART TWO: LEADERSHIP FROM A TO Z (WITH AN EMPHASIS ON C)

CHAPTER THREE

The First Essential—
The Necessity of Change 61

CHAPTER FOUR

The Second Essential—
The Psychology of Change 81

CHAPTER FIVE

The Third Essential—
The Factors of Condition 101

CHAPTER SIX

The Fourth Essential—
The Foundations of Capital 121

CHAPTER SEVEN

The Fifth Essential—
The Magic of Connection 139

CHAPTER EIGHT

The Sixth Essential—
The Misfortune of Collapse 157

CHAPTER NINE

The Seventh Essential—
The Importance of Continuation 179

PART THREE: APPLICATION

CHAPTER TEN

Ernest Shackleton Case Study
in Ideal Leadership 201

CHAPTER ELEVEN

Ideal Leadership Development
Plan (ILDP) Workbook 211

Ideal Leadership Series 221

Foreword

What exactly makes a great leader? This should be an easy question to answer. After all, we have had countless number of great leaders as role models over the centuries in every domain of life. Yet the experts on the subject of leadership cannot manage to agree on any definite pattern to what it takes to lead effectively.

I witnessed this firsthand during a top-level leadership course in December 2002. I was attending a weeklong seminar entitled, "Leadership in the 21st Century" at the Kennedy School of Government at Harvard University. Attendance was limited to a handpicked assortment of government leaders, business heads, and directors of nonprofit organizations from all over the world. Our seminar featured a number of experts in the field of leadership including the noted author Ronald Heifetz and presidential advisor David Gergen.

It was a Friday, the last day of our seminar, and I was at the dining hall with an early-morning group of seminar attendees. There were about eight of us who liked to get an early start on the day and eat breakfast as soon as the kitchen crew was ready. We had finished eating and were idly chatting when I asked the group about their impressions after a week of lectures and discussions. Everyone agreed that it was a rewarding experience due to the networking and sharing. Then I asked, "Can anyone tell me one new thing that you learned this week about leadership?" It suddenly got very quiet. Each person looked at the others and waited for a response—but no one had an answer.

I then commented that perhaps it was because our speakers, un-questionably brilliant and professional in their respective fields, were operating from a post-modern perspective. From their view, it was up to us to make the discoveries and not be spoon-fed some preconceived notions. I remarked, rather honestly, that this approach was not what I expected. I had not spent thousands of dollars and a week of valuable time to simply be told that I had to find answers within myself.

My colleagues reluctantly agreed. They admitted that their motiva-tion in attending this particular seminar at Harvard was because they felt that what they desperately needed was some structure that they could build their leadership knowledge upon. I mentioned that I had been teaching leadership in the Baltic countries, and had developed such a structure that many leaders there had found helpful.

I pulled out a napkin and drew a pyramid on it. I showed how the base of the pyramid represented the "Leadership Conditions," the parameters necessary for an individual to have the opportunity to lead others. The top of the pyramid consisted of six competencies that I called "Leadership Capital." I explained that these determine how effective an individual will be in leading an organization forward in a positive direction. For several minutes I gave them the essence of what I called the "Ideal Leadership Model" and how it could be used as a guide for lifelong learning in leadership.

One of the group members, a director for a center for delinquent youth in Harlem, was clearly impressed. He asked if he could keep the napkin and even if I would sign it. Then, as we were leaving the cafeteria to prepare for the last seminar sessions, he turned to me and pointed to the napkin and said, "Larry, you need to write a book about this."

Since that time I have had the opportunity to travel to a number of countries and speak with hundreds of leaders in all walks of life. I hear the same cry everywhere—there is so much information about leadership, but we don't know how all the pieces fit together. Though the gurus at Harvard and other academic institutions may not be able to understand this, leaders who are in the trenches of everyday grind need something practical to live by. Whether we recognize it or not, we are looking for some framework that is practicable to use and yet complete enough to deal with the many complexities of today's world. This book is being written with that need in mind.

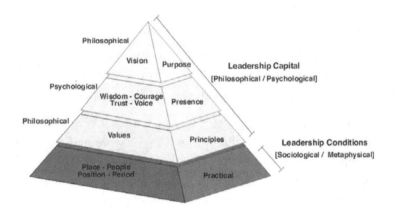

I know that there are only two reasons why a person would want to read a book on leadership: either they are a leader, or they want to be one. Both groups have much in common. For those currently serving in some leadership capacity or another, there is a very good chance that this is not the first book that has been read on the subject of leadership. Many managers and directors pursue leadership literature in the hopes that they may get a good pointer or two. I had one company owner tell me that he discovered a "$100,000 idea" every time he heard me lecture. (I told him that I wanted a finder's fee!) Often just one good idea can make a big difference in directing others, so a conscientious leader often searches diligently to find that single, great, breakthrough idea.

However, this book is very different. It is not designed to give good ideas; it is designed to give a good design! Specifically, it presents the Ideal Leadership Model. This runs against many leadership programs that suggest that a person must design his or her own personal leadership model. The beauty of the Ideal Leadership Model is that it does not negate this pursuit. The model presented in this book is a completely comprehensive one. Every single leader can find something within it to build on.

This might not be what the reader has in mind, of course. However, I am asking that we strip down our thinking to the bone, and get back to the very essentials. For many, it seems I am asking them to buy a new car when all they want is a little tune-up on the old one. But the extra investment in time and mental energy could be well worth the effort. Getting a brand-new perspective may open up completely new avenues that were never dreamed of before.

The questions at the end of each chapter, listed under "Active Leaders," are for those who are currently in a position of influence over others. Think about the answers. Talk them over with a mentor or fellow traveler along the road of leadership development. Make your learning active!

Attention: FLOWters (**F**uture **L**eaders **o**f the **W**orld). A word to those who are aspiring leaders—this may very well be the first book you are reading on the subject of leadership. In my 30 years of teaching, I have come to realize that no subject in the field of psychology is more difficult for secondary and undergraduate students to grasp than leadership in the abstract. It is a lot like parenthood; every child thinks he will improve on his own parents' efforts until he actually starts having children and then realizes just how tough it really is to be a parent!

The first chapter, "Understanding the Mystery," was written particularly with students in mind.

The reason why introductory courses at the university always start with foundational material, such as the terminology and philosophy of the discipline, is because that stuff is important. Once the foundations are clearly understood, then it is possible to do some further study in the field. I believe students have much to contribute to the world of leadership development.

Remember the Hermeneutical Circle—the paradox that states to understand the particulars of an idea, one must see it in its entirety, yet to see it in its entirety requires understanding the particulars. This book will hopefully help the leader of the future see the forest and the trees at the same time. The benefit of starting with the Ideal Leadership Model, is that once it is understood, the mystery will disappear from the idea of what makes a good leader and what a person has to do to become one. It can provide an excellent foundation to a road of lifetime learning in leadership for those willing to make that journey.

Understanding leadership is not as difficult as brain surgery, but it is necessary to open up the brain to get it!

Larry W. Stout, Dr.Ph.D., MBA
Associate Professor of Psychology
Stockholm School of Economics in Riga

PART ONE

What Is Leadership?

CHAPTER ONE

Understanding the Mystery—Why Leadership Doesn't Make Sense

True Blue

Leadership is a mystery. Although anyone can recognize a leader when he sees one, the identification of the leadership process itself remains an elusive enigma. Rabbi Daniel Lapin said it best when he asked, "Why does everyone agree on how to produce top-rate doctors, car mechanics, and physicists, but nobody seems to agree on how to produce top-rate leaders? Medical education in Bombay does not differ substantially from medical training in Boston; but every single leadership training program claims to have its own unique system."[1] After decades of research and writing, there is still no clear picture anywhere of how to understand leadership. With over 2,000 books written per year on the subject of leadership, each with a different perspective, it is fair to ask the question, "Who is right?"

So before we can concretely outline yet *another* leadership design, we will justify why we think this is the right one. For those who are not concerned about this, jump ahead to Chapter Two and begin to read how to unravel the mystery using the seven essential leadership concepts. For those who are still with us, though, let's walk step-by-step through the process so that it will be crystal clear why the Ideal Leadership Model can work better than any other and why it is so important.

The lack of consensus in the subject of *leadership* is not quite so surprising, given that it is a relatively new word in the English vocabulary, first appearing in a letter about British politics in 1821. However, the word *leader* appears in a variety of places in literature as far back as the 12th century in a variety of contexts; the leader of an army, one who guides others, a person who is head of government, enterprise or movement, etc. Leaders were around for centuries before anyone started seriously thinking about what it meant to be one!

Obviously, it is easier to comprehend something concrete (such as leaders) than it is an abstract concept (such as leadership). One of the beauties of the Hebrew language is that it uses concrete images to convey abstract thoughts, such as *wind* and *breath* for the word *spirit*. When God is spoken of as the Holy Spirit, it conveys both a sense of unseen power (wind) but also a personalized presence (breath). The concrete imagery conveys deeper spiritual truths.

Hebrew word imagery can be helpful in examining leadership. Here is an exercise that seems deceptively simple, but is actually quite difficult: Describe the color *blue* without using it as an adjective. (Think about that for a moment.) Our minds instantly think of blue sky, blue jeans, blue crayons, maybe even the *Blue Boy* painting by Gainsborough. This happens for two reasons. First, we know what blue is, but only when it is in context with something. Blue, as an independent entity, is almost impossible to describe outside of highly technical language relating to light frequencies. Normally, our minds immediately associate it with an object. Why we picked that particular object is the second factor; our perspective affects our understanding. If we knew of only one blue object in our entire existence, then the "blueness" of that object would determine our understanding of the color.

The same difficulty relates to leadership. Say the word *leadership* and we picture in our mind certain leaders—ones who from our perspective represent this concept. But the leaders do not describe *leadership* anymore than blue jeans describe the color blue. The objects relate to the color; they do not define it. This is why James MacGregor Burns famously stated that "leadership is the most observed and least understood phenomenon in the world."[2]

But unlike a primary color, leadership is more like a rainbow of colors—a diffusion of light that forms different patterns under different conditions. As we will see, these different colors will represent the competencies of leadership, which we call *Leadership Capital* and the environment in which they exist, which we call *Leadership Conditions*.

To take the analogy one step further, a rainbow can be described in different ways depending on the perspective of the one describing it.

> To the scientist Arthur Eddington, "a rainbow, described in the symbolism of physics is a band of aetherial vibrations arranged in systematic order of wave-length from about .000040 cm to .000072 cm."

> To the poet William Wordsworth, "My heart leaps up when I behold a rainbow in the sky; So was it when my life began; So is it now I am a man; So let it be when I shall grow old, or let me die!"

> To the Bible writer, "And God said, *'This is the sign of the covenant I am making between Me and you and every living creature with you, a covenant for all generations to come: I have set My rainbow in the clouds, and it will be the sign of the covenant between Me and the earth"* (Gen. 9:12-13).

The rainbow is to one an atmospheric optical phenomena, to another a work of art, and to another a promise of God. And they all are right! A rainbow is not one thing; it has many facets depending on the one looking at it.

This is our approach to the subject of leadership. A psychologist considers the problem-solving, strategic-thinking processes on one side, as well as the interpersonal dynamics of the leader; a philosopher focuses on the overall philosophical orientation of the leader; whereas a sociologist examines the various conditions that cause one to be in leadership and not another.

Because there are many disciplines interacting in the process of leadership, we choose to call this the "Interdisciplinary Leadership Model." A shortened form takes the **I** from Inter, the **D** from Disciplinary, and adds the **L** of Leadership to form the word *Ideal*. We believe that all leadership, when it occurs, is in the form of the "Ideal Leadership Model."

The word "Ideal" was chosen for more than its use as an acronym. In Greek, there is a word *arête*, which is an almost untranslatable term referring to the Platonic idea of forms. Plato theorized that there was an ideal form, *arête*, for everything we see on earth. So, the reason we can look at many different kinds of dogs and still know they are dogs is because there is, somewhere (Plato never said where), a form of an ideal dog that we compare each earthly dog to.

Of course, we know from cognitive psychology today that this is not how our minds associate information, but the principle is still useful for our discussion. There are hundreds of different types of dogs, and though they all are quite different from one another, they still have a "dogginess" about them that causes us to know what they are. However, when we see a wolf, we see something different. The wolf has many "doggy" features; yet there is a difference about it, and we instinctively know it is something else.

This is our approach to leadership. We are setting up the parameters of what we believe leadership to be, which we are calling the Ideal Leadership Model. We are not saying that a person must be ideal to be a leader. Rather, we are saying that when a person is truly acting as a leader, we recognize them as such because they follow the design in the Ideal Model.

Just as wolves are not dogs, so there are those who resemble leaders but are actually not. We will term these individuals "anti-leaders." Wolves have a strong predator instinct and are almost impossible to domesticate. Anti-leaders are not ones who seek to develop and enhance the group they represent; rather they are motivated largely by self-centered interests. (This is only for the purpose of analogy. We have nothing personal against wolves; we just would not want one for a pet!)

When we use the word *Ideal*, we are referring to the *arête* of leadership. If that is true, then it should also adequately define *leadership* wherever it occurs. So if there is a leader in a small business, or in the army, or in the Boy Scouts, or in an inner-city school, they fit the design of Ideal Leadership. Also, this implies that the model should be applicable to leaders during any time period. In other words, what is blue is blue no matter who wears it or when they wear it.

But in saying this, we are not saying that all other theorists about leadership have been wrong. Quite the contrary, we want to show that, in most cases, they all were right. The way this is possible is by understanding another aspect of science—the quest for the unified theory.

One Size Fits All

Perhaps *leadership theory* could take a hint from the world of physics. For years, physicists have been seeking to unify the two foundational pillars upon which modern physics rests: general relativity and quantum mechanics. These theories have produced unimaginable accuracy in virtually all their predictions, but as Brian Greene explains, there is one big problem, "As they are currently formulated, general relativity and quantum mechanics *cannot both be right*.

> "The two theories underlying the tremendous progress of physics during the last hundred years—progress that has explained the expansion of the heavens and the fundamental structure of matter—are mutually incompatible" (emphasis, Brian Greene).[3]

Understand what Greene is saying here. There are two theories—one for the world of the microscope and the other for the world of telescope, and these theories have served each of these worlds very well. As Greene notes, physicists have experimentally confirmed with uncanny accuracy virtually all predictions made by each of these theories. Because these two disciplines rarely, if ever, interact with each other, the fact that these theories contradict has not been of particular concern.

This incompatibility has driven scientists since the time of Albert Einstein to seek for one unifying theory that would encompass all the current models. In recent years, superstring theory has been suggested as an answer. Because this new theory encompasses the vast expanse of space as well as the world of the subatomic particle and everything in between, it has been called the Theory of Everything.

The Theory of Everything seeks to show how both contradictory theories can still be true. (We are not stating if the theory works or not, simply that it serves the purpose of unifying physics.) This is what we are endeavoring to do with the Ideal Leadership Model. We want to demonstrate that it is a unifying theory; all the various explanations for leadership, legitimate within their scope, can be encompassed in this model. In addition, this one model will also serve to explain leadership in all its domains: political leadership, military leadership, business leadership, sports leadership, spiritual leadership, etc. It will also explain leadership in all times in history. In other words, we are endeavoring in this model to explain leadership, period. Whenever and wherever it is found—be it an Isaac Newton, Mahatma Gandhi, or Henry Ford—it will resemble the Ideal Leadership Model.

Perhaps we could use an analogy to the game of baseball. Various baseball players who have excelled at the game write how best to hit the ball, run the bases, play in the field, etc. They have different styles, of course; and in reading different accounts, a person who wants to play the game can discover some good ideas for himself. Let's further imagine that there are those who have never actually played, but have studied the game for a long time and also have good suggestions on the best skills for playing baseball.

This is exactly the situation we have in leadership studies. Many people are writing and talking about how best to play the game, *but there is no agreement on exactly what constitutes the game itself!* This is what the Ideal Leadership Model endeavors to do—define the game. We hope to outline the parameters in their essence so that all the suggestions on skills and techniques and strategy begin to make sense.

I use the baseball analogy on purpose. For several years, I attempted to teach the incoming students at Stockholm School of Economics in Riga the game of baseball. I would go over the fundamentals in class, and then we would go to a football field and mark out the field so we could play the game. More times than not, the results were pretty disastrous. I had grown up playing the game and never realized how complex this simple kid's game was to play for those who had no idea of the basics.

Some of the students could hit and run and catch quite well, but these skills had no real value unless they were integrated into the proper way to play the game. We had lots of fun, but we could hardly call it "playing baseball." It would probably be more accurately described as playing with a baseball.

This is the situation concerning leadership studies. We have many excellent teachers telling us about skills, but what has been missing is a comprehensive picture (the game itself) of leadership. This is what we believe is presented with the Ideal Leadership Model. It explains the game. It defines what leadership is and what it is not. We have seen in training sessions with many managers and leaders, that when they grasp the idea, they have an "aha" experience. It is like they have been watching the game of baseball for years, but now for the first time, they understand it.

What exactly are we referring to when we speak of a "model?" Scientists use the term to refer to a particular framework that explains a phenomenon being studied. Let me use an analogy based on a humorous experience I had when I first began to work in Latvia in 1991. I was invited to give an introductory lecture on Western teaching methodologies at the six pedagogical institutes (teacher colleges) in the country. I decided to visit the ones furthest away from the capital city of Riga first, so I traveled west to the coastal city of Liepaja and spoke at their school. The next week I traveled southeast to the city of Daugavpils. When I stood in front of the school there, I thought I was experiencing *déjà vu*. It was exactly the same building! I discovered that in the Soviet system, there was one design for a pedagogical academy. When my escort invited to take me to the rector's office, I told her she did not need to bother because I knew exactly where the office was located. And I was right.

Now, let us use this as an illustration for leadership. When I see that particular style of building, I know when I enter that I am in a pedagogical institute. It is a model that is used for that purpose. So it is, when we hold up our model, known as Ideal Leadership, we will know that those who fit that picture are leaders.

What happens when we do not have a model? Well, let us imagine that a group of students do not know which building represents a pedagogical institute. They are told it has pillars in the front, so one finds an arts building, another finds a courthouse, and another finds a city hall. They all have similar features to the pedagogical institute, but that does not make them one. The students are given another piece of information—the pedagogical institute has a large lecture hall on one floor and smaller lecture rooms on two other floors. Now, half the students find it, but the other half find themselves at an after-school recreation center.

But if the students are shown a picture of the outside and a blueprint of the inside, they cannot be mistaken. They will find the right place. This is what a good model does; it presents a complete picture. We will not get lost and we will not end up in the wrong place. This explains why over the years we have had an amazing amount of good information about leadership, yet leadership itself still remains such a mystery.

Mystery Writers

Though there seems to be a wide variety of topics on the subject, contemporary leadership books and articles fall into five general categories. Some of these combine the categories, but most generally seem to be exclusive to one main area.

The first is ***historical reflection***. These are books that look back in history and attempt to explain why George Washington or Napoleon Bonaparte was so effective (or ineffective) as a leader. The content of these books is generally a selective biography of the leader or leaders being studied, followed with some nuggets of insight thrown in here and there. These books are popular because the stories are almost always interesting and easy to read, and they also do not make many demands upon the reader.

It would seem that history is the best way to study leadership, because as George Santayana wrote in 1905, "Those who cannot remember the past are condemned to repeat it." But, unfortunately, the problem with the historical reflection method is to find what part of the past we are to remember. What "lessons from history" are universal? The authors of leadership history strain to make the connections to the present, but they cannot make the connection to each other. Even a comparison between two of the greatest American presidents, Abraham Lincoln and George Washington, reveals two completely different leaders in their personalities, styles of directing and leading others, as well as in their communication skills and techniques.

Past experience should be a guidepost, not a hitching post. History illustrates, but it does not illuminate. Historians Richard E. Neustadt and Ernest R. May concluded, "We wish we could suggest a mini-method the decision-maker could reliably employ in juggling the relationships (between the past and the present). We cannot. This brings us to the absolute frontier of our considerations and experiments up till now. We have no more to offer than a general attitude, a cast of mind, an outlook, not a method—along with our tests for presumptions. Time is viewed as though it were a stream."[4] If those who are experts in history will not make the claim that historical reflection can be used as a model, those who are knowledgeable in leadership should take heed.

The second type of leadership book is somewhat similar to the historical reflection type, but it focuses on the successful contemporary leader. These could be termed leadership examples by **anecdotal experience**. Virtually every successful business executive, salesperson, politician, movie star, recording artist, athletic champion, or hero-of-the-moment feels the need to preserve his or her achievements for posterity through the written word. These books are popular because there is a natural curiosity about successful people, especially those with whom we are most familiar. We often feel we know these people somehow and enjoy reading the inside information about their lives.

But the same problem listed under historical reflection is again evidenced here. What universal applications can be derived from these various "success" stories? Hindsight is an exact science, but unfortunately, we do not live that way. There is also the problem that any account of an individual's life is somewhat biased. Again, to quote Neustadt and May, "Personal records are prey to gaps, mistakes, and misunderstandings.

Inferences are but hypotheses, not even easily substantiated, let alone 'proved.'"[5]

One step above the anecdotal experience, which usually focuses on one person or company, are leadership books about the **best practices**. This type of book burst on the scene with Tom Peters and Robert Waterman's 1982 bestseller, *In Search of Excellence: Lessons from America's Best Run Companies* (Warner Books).

These two consultants from McKinsey & Company conducted a research project from 1979 to 1980 in which they investigated the qualities common to the best-run companies in America. After selecting a sample of 43 successful American companies from six major industries, they examined the firms' practices closely and came up with a model of eight core principles for excellence.

The book literally rocked the business world. It was a *New York Times* bestseller for over three years and eventually sold over six million copies, at the time the most successful business book ever. Further, the "best practices" concept virtually created the business guru industry. Before this time, those who were considered management experts simply wrote articles in academic journals, gave the occasional seminar, and worked as consultants for a few large corporations. Only the biggest blockbusters sold more than a few hundred thousand books.

Today, the management guru business (with Tom Peters still one of the top figures) is a billion dollar industry, and anyone who is anyone has a book attesting to his or her wisdom and expertise. Best practices types of books are routinely on the bestseller lists. They usually document a particular industry or group of industries that have "done it right," often based on insight from the author of the book.

Related to the best practices, but not quite of the intellectual stature, are the leadership books that could be called **simple solutions**. These books feature gurus who simply compile the work of others and come up with seven pillars of success or ten proven points of leadership effectiveness. They often include exciting examples with large print and many clever eye-catching illustrations, which make them quick reads. Usually popular in airport bookstores, they appeal to the busy business manager who is looking for some pointers and hints on being better or more effective in his or her job. These books are obviously not of high literary caliber, but they do not aim at an academic market. They are written by people in the "real world" who have discovered how to make things happen and get things done.

The best practices books serve a useful purpose because, like *In Search of Excellence,* they are generally well researched and the principles they outline are systematically identified. They also generally illustrate the author's key points with good stories. The simple solutions books often take principles down one more step of simplicity, reducing the best practices to a few, easy-to-remember, key points.

However, the same arguments used against the first two types of books must be made about these two types also. Though *In Search of Excellence* is still read and quoted, some of the examples of successful companies used in the book such as Digital and Wang did not even make it intact through the decade of the 1980s. The simple solution books propose universal truths, but they only offer anecdotal evidence and a patchwork of information from various sources, many times contradictory and sometimes even false. These are "fun" books: easy to read, easy to understand, and not meant to be taken too seriously.

The final types of books are the **scientific studies**. These are the books that quote numerous research studies to support certain ideas or concepts. This is what is generally thought of as "serious" leadership literature.

However, despite the voluminous number of studies conducted regarding leadership over the years, no clear picture of leadership has emerged. Daniel Goleman wrote for *Harvard Business Review* in the year 2000 that "there is virtually no quantitative research that has demonstrated which precise leadership behaviors yield positive results."[6]

In the absence of consensus, there are innumerable competing theories. David Gergen, professor at the John F. Kennedy School of Government at Harvard University and speechwriter for three U.S. presidents, estimates that there are some 250 different models for leadership.

Bernard Bass, the author of the *Bass and Stogdill's Handbook on Leadership* ("the indispensable 'bible' for every serious student of leadership," according to the cover fly-leaf) states that there are almost as many different definitions of *leadership* as there are persons who have attempted to define the concept.

Searching for a clear answer to the mystery of leadership almost resembles the quest for the philosopher's stone or the Holy Grail in the Middle Ages. In the May 30, 2000, issue of the *International Herald Tribune* there was a report that, "In the spring of 2000, a conference at Harvard University jointly sponsored by the John F. Kennedy School of Government and the world leadership group of the InterAction Council bogged down immediately as a few dozen well-practiced minds came up with endless answers." The article was entitled, "Leadership is All the Rage, But Few Know What It Is."

Needed: A Good Theory

It should not be misunderstood that all these books and articles and ideas that have been circulating for years have been to no avail. Indeed, it is almost impossible not to pick up at least one good suggestion from most popular leadership books or articles. Many good ideas came out of all this study and research, and much of it has become standard practice in most businesses and industries today. But as has been mentioned previously, none of the research conclusively shows the key components of leadership.

The reason is that the experts have been trying to describe a phenomenon not unlike the blind men and the elephant. There is a legend from India of the blind men who came upon an elephant. As each one examined a part of the elephant, they mistakenly related it to something that they already understood. One touched the legs and thought an elephant was like a tree; one touched the body and thought an elephant was like a wall; another touched the tusk and thought it was like a spear; while still another feeling the tail felt an elephant was like a rope. The poet John G. Saxe stated it well when he wrote, "And so these men of Indostan disputed loud and long, each in his own opinion exceeding stiff and strong; though each was partly in the right, and all were in the wrong."

The problem is one that is common in teaching—the paradox of the Hermeneutical Circle. It states that to understand the particulars of an idea, one must see it in its entirety, yet to see it in its entirety requires understanding the particulars. It is like the philosophy professor who told his class about Plato's *Republic*, "You have to slug through it a couple of times before you can really read it once."

Until the whole picture is understood, the particulars do not make much sense. But to get to that point, the particulars must be put together into one picture!

So what scientists do to get around this paradox is to conceptualize what they think the elephant does look like. Kurt Lewin noted, "There is nothing so practical as a good theory." Although George Box sarcastically commented, "All models are wrong. Some models are useful." Thomas Kuhn, in his brilliant analysis of the working of scientific investigation, termed these working assumptions "paradigms." He took the word from the Greek word *paradigma*, which is a word describing a pattern or map for understanding and explaining certain aspects of reality. Kuhn notes that before "normal science" can be conducted, the experts must have a common reference set (a paradigm), which can be used to explain and predict the phenomenon being studied.[7]

Now, if we apply this to the study of leadership, we are saying that there must be some standard model that can be universally applied, and simply conducting studies of leaders to arrive at this standard will never work. Why? Let's use an example of a very good study and try to establish a paradigm from it.

The Gallup Organization recently conducted a study of 5,019 leaders from a wide range of industries and sectors, including education, healthcare, the military, government, finance, insurance, and retail. Gallup is a highly reputable organization, and we can be sure that they conducted this research with the utmost integrity and attention to statistical analysis and validity. Their research led them to conclude that there were seven "demands" of leadership. These include visioning, maximizing values, challenging experience, mentoring, building a constituency, making sense of experience, and knowing self.[8]

Let us assume for the moment that Gallup has it exactly right—they have hit the nail on the head; these are the seven universal demands that compose the activity of a leader. Yet like so many other studies as such, this answers one question about leadership (What was the right combination of factors that cause a person to successfully lead an organization?) but opens the door to other questions. For example:

- Are these factors equally important at all times in the leader's tenure?

- Why do some seem to lead effectively for a while, and then fail later?

- How does one maintain his leadership capabilities?

- Where do leaders come from? Are they born with these attributes, or are they bred?

- If these demands of leadership are not gender specific, why are there not more female leaders?

Gallup has provided good market research about present leaders in a number of different domains. It is also true that these seven "demands" are certainly a good reflection of leadership. But can it be used as a template for the study of all leadership? Where does "visioning" come from? What happens if a leader is excellent in "knowing self" but weak in sharing it with others, the "mentoring" aspect? The study works for what it studied, but to provide a broader application, something else is needed.

In the final analysis, a good theory of leadership must be able to withstand scientific scrutiny. Any good theory of leadership must have three dimensions: It should be able to completely describe a leader, tell what it takes to become one, and predict those who will be leaders.

*A true leadership theory or model must be **descriptive**.* This means that the idea or theory must fully describe the complete phenomenon displayed by the leader. This is what all studies in leadership maintain they do, but actually this is more complex than it might at first appear. Consider again the previous example about two of the greatest U.S. presidents, George Washington and Abraham Lincoln. George Washington was born into a wealthy family; Abraham Lincoln was born in a log cabin on the American frontier. Washington had an excellent education; Lincoln was primarily self-educated. Washington was a man of few words, noted for his serious demeanor; Lincoln was well-spoken and had a wonderful sense of humor. The differences between these men go on and on.

These two great American presidents could not have been more different in the way they became leaders, their particular leadership style, and the way that they influenced people. Any theory, whether it is Gallup's Seven Demands, Covey's Seven Habits,[9] or Maxwell's Twenty-One Irrefutable Laws,[10] must be inclusive enough to explain these differences. Too often, they do not. If they did, they could also be used for prescriptive purposes.

*A true leadership theory or model must be **prescriptive***. The present studies conducted on leaders show us the final product—the leaders who have made it to the top. But what of those who are not there but are aspiring to get to the top? This, of course, is the whole idea behind the idea of best practices. If a person applies the best practices, he will succeed. The difficulty with the present, best-practice models is that they are not truly prescriptive.

A couple of years ago, I had a terrible stomachache as well as pains in my arms and legs. I went to the hospital, and the staff conducted a number of tests but were unable to find what was wrong with me. They were stumped because they had never seen such an odd set of symptoms. Finally, one astute doctor realized that the difficulty in diagnosis was that they were looking for a single, solitary explanation for my pains, when in fact, I had contracted *two* diseases simultaneously. Shortly after, the doctors were able to prescribe the right treatment, and I made an immediate recovery.

In leadership, there is rarely a single key that will catapult an individual into leadership success. By establishing a standard that can be compared to in its entirety, a proper plan of action can be established. A person needs to be able to crawl before he can walk and walk before he can run, so to speak. A good leadership model assists the aspiring leader in identifying exactly where he is on the path toward ideal leadership and exactly how to get there.

*A true leadership theory or model must be **predictive***. This is the most glaring omission from virtually all books on leadership. How can leadership be identified before a person becomes one? Good science is predictive; the reason we know a theory is true is because it can be applied in situations where the conditions exist, and the results will be known before they occur.

Albert Einstein theorized the Special Theory of Relativity, then devised a rigorous set of tests to prove its validity. Paul Johnson wrote that the modern world began on 29 May 1919, because this was the day that solar-eclipse expeditions tested and proved Einstein's predictions of light-deflection at twice the rate that classical Newtonian theory would have predicted.[11] Though Einstein's theory flew in the face of the accepted laws of physics of the previous two hundred years, it was accepted because it was shown to be more accurate predicatively.

Predictiveness is a most important consideration for those working in developing nations where there are not role models of leaders. They have to rise up—but from where? Who? It is one thing to write that leaders must be visionary, but how can that vision be recognized in an individual before he needs it? All leadership theorists agree on the importance of courage, but what is the embryo of courage in a leader?

Because my wife works as a nurse at the United States Embassy in Riga, I occasionally have the opportunity to have lunch with her there. Once, we were sitting with a colonel from the U.S. Marine Corps, and I asked him that very question. I wondered how the Marines, which epitomize courage in action, are able to tell which recruits have it and which ones do not before they must display it under fire? He told me honestly that they do not know. They just count on the training the Marines give them to get them through the crisis.

So in the U.S. Marines Corps' case, courage comes from confidence. Develop more confidence and the individual Marine will have more courage. Yet we all know from experience that some people seem to have a reservoir of courage that cannot be simply explained from experience. Where does it come from?

The reason why these questions are important is because if we cannot identify these embryonic elements of leadership, there is no way we can truly develop them. Without a given model that can explain the structure of leadership development, we are left with a useless circular reasoning model. A person becomes a leader because he has the capacity to become one, and the reason he has the capacity is because he is a leader.

No, that will not do. A good leadership theory should not only tell us who leaders are and how they can develop, but also help us to know who will be leaders in the future. In plain language, it is not difficult after the sports contest is over to explain why one team beat another, but it is of greater benefit to be able to do that analysis *before* the contest and accurately predict the winner.

It is the predictive element of a scientific theory that gives it credence. If any combinations of factors are truly indicative of leadership, then they should exist in some embryo state in the leader-in-the-making.

This puts the bar up very high. But we were placed in a situation where the present offerings in leadership theory were not effective enough. Forged out of the pressures of discovering and developing leadership in a newly emerging democratic republic, the Ideal Leadership Model had to meet the criteria of a good theory.

In addition, we did not have the luxury of offering up some esoteric academic jargon to the society in which we were working.

In every domain—government, business, education, finance, the arts, even religion—leaders were desperately needed to move past the rigidity of the Soviet mind-set. Latvia, Lithuania, and Estonia wanted to join the West, and they knew that it would come only when leaders stepped up and provided the right direction.

After years of practical application, we believe it is ready to be offered to a wider venue than the Baltic countries. Whether we have discovered the model for leadership, only time will tell. This is where the road begins, though. And maybe at the end of the road, there is a rainbow.

Endnotes

1. Lapin, Daniel, *Thou Shalt Prosper* (John Wiley & Sons, New York, NY, 2005),173.

2. Burns, James MacGregor, *Leadership* (Harper Perennial, London, UK, 1982).

3. Greene, Brian, *The Elegant Universe: Superstrings, Hidden Dimensions, and the Quest for the Ultimate Theory* (Vintage Books, New York, NY, 2003), 3.

4. Neustadt, Richard E. and May, Ernest R., *Thinking in Time: The Uses of History for Decision-Makers* (Free Press, 1986), 237.

5. Ibid.

6. Goleman, Daniel, "Leadership That Gets Results", *Harvard Business Review* (March-April 2000), 78.

7. Kuhn, Thomas. *Structure of Scientific Revolutions, 3rd ed.*, (University of Chicago Press, Chicago, IL, 1997).

8. Conchie, Barry, "The Seven Demands of Leadership: What separates great leaders from all the rest" *Gallup Management Journal* (May 2004), 1-4.

9. Covey, Stephen R., *The Seven Habits of Highly Effective People* (Simon & Schuster, New York, NY, 1989).

10. Maxwell, John, *The 21 Irrefutable Laws of Leadership* (Thomas Nelson, Inc, Nashville, TN, 1998).

11. Johnson, Paul. *Modern Times: The World from the Twenties to the Eighties*, (Harper & Row, London, UK, 1983).

Key Ideas

1. Leadership is an abstract concept that we use to describe the concrete reality we see in leaders.

2. The leadership genre presents many facets of leadership, and has been explained using historical reflection, anecdotal experiences, best practices, simple solutions, and scientific studies.

3. Study without a grounding theory does not provide a comprehensive picture. Leadership research without a theory produces as many questions as it answers.

4. Good leadership theory must be scientific, meaning it must be descriptive, prescriptive, and predictive.

Questions for Active Leaders

1. What defines a "good" book on the subject of leadership? Is it because it provides inspiration, or instruction, or a combination of both?

2. What is the biggest difficulty in applying ideas from leadership books? Why?

Questions for FLOWters (Future Leaders of the World)

1. Try to describe "leadership." How is this different than simply describing a leader?

2. If asked to assist in developing a good working theory on leadership, what should be the most important consideration? That it would be simple? Practical? Effective? Complete?

CHAPTER TWO

Unraveling the Mystery— The Ideal Leadership Model

Up the Elevator

A colleague from Ireland, Bill Barbour, sat in my office and asked, "So Larry, exactly what is so unique about your leadership model?" My fellow professor has taught leadership in many universities in Europe and as far away as China, so he knows quite a bit about this subject. What Bill expected me to give him was the "elevator speech." In the time it takes an elevator to go up to the top floor (generally considered somewhere between 16 and 60 seconds), the main concepts of an idea are presented. In this fast-paced world, we want and need these content-rich nuggets of information. These short capsules tell us what we need and nothing more. Spare me the details and give me the bottom line—that is the business card being requested today.

So I told him, "True leaders move their organizations forward in a positive direction. They have six key competencies paired around the three primary functions of a leader. The philosophy or ideology is drawn from their *vision* and *values*; their personal traits for problem-solving and decision-making from their *wisdom* and *courage*; and their interpersonal attributes of working with others from their trust and voice.

These are known as their 'Leadership Capital,' but these need to be activated by the 'Leadership Conditions' of being at the right place, at the right time, doing the right things with the right people. Deficiencies in either Capital or Conditions will prevent real leadership from taking place or result in its opposite—anti-leadership."

I could see the wheels turning in my esteemed colleague's head, as he quickly processed this concept against the many other ideas he knew about leadership. He began to realize the implications and immediately started peppering me with questions. But as I have shared the elevator speech with others who have less of a breadth in the leadership genre, they look at me with a small sense of bewilderment and ask, "So how does it work?"

This is a different question than the first one. It requires another trip up the elevator (or maybe down!). To understand how it works requires going step-by-step through leadership progression. This working process is what I have termed the "Seven Leadership Essentials" or even more simply, "Leadership in Seven Sentences." They are as follows:

1. Leadership implies change and initiating change.
2. Any change must benefit the followers and not just the leader.
3. The right Conditions must exist to initiate a change.
4. Success in leading depends on a leader's Capital.
5. Success in leadership happens when Conditions and Capital coincide.
6. Failure in leadership is a result of changing Conditions or misapplied Capital.
7. Leadership Capital is an expendable resource.

Taking each one of these sentences and building on it provides a comprehensive picture of leadership in the context of the Ideal Model. In fact, everything we will ever learn about leadership can be categorized under one of these seven subheadings.

Leadership in Seven Sentences

---

1. Leadership implies change and initiating change.

Management is maintaining the organization, keeping everything running smoothly; whereas leaders push to make changes—they go beyond status quo. Leaders, by definition, lead.

Because it is often difficult to grasp a new concept, it is useful to define what it is not. In examining leadership, it is often compared with management. Volumes have been written about the difference between leaders and managers but what usually is remembered is pithy little sayings like, "Managers do things right whereas leaders do the right things." What is often implied is that there is something disparaging about a manager. They are "B List" people, not "A List." In truth, no organization would last very long if it did not have good, solid managers maintaining the operational systems and processes.

Imagine a simple little grocery shop on the corner called Frank's Fresh Foods managed by a smart store manager named Peter. We walk in and notice that it is clean, laid out nicely, and the stock is clearly marked and represents an ample variety of choices of goods. The staff is friendly and helpful, and we discover further that the store turns a good profit. We would say that this is a well-managed shop. Peter, the manager responsible for the operation of this enterprise, has maximized his finances, facility, and human resources in such a way that he sells the maximum volume of products possible. He is a good manager.

Every organization needs these individuals. They *know* the business. They know how to get the most out of the least. They understand how the systems should work and know how to get their staff to follow these systems. It often takes an individual years to become extremely proficient at doing this, which is why good managers are so highly prized in any company or enterprise.

But let us further imagine that a new store opens right across the street—the SuperDuper Market. It has a larger sales area, a wider selection, and better prices than Frank's Fresh Foods. There is a very good chance that this nice well-managed shop will lose customers and perhaps over time be driven out of business. What happened? Quite simply, the environment changed. Maintaining status quo is acceptable only when the environment is also status quo. Unfortunately, in real life, this rarely happens.

The owner of the corner shop, Frank himself, must now take on the mantle of leadership for his very survival. Frank studies the situation and sees a new vision for his company. SuperDuper Market will focus on the masses, but Frank's Fresh Foods will be marketed completely differently.

He instructs Peter that the shop will now institute some new services, such as home grocery delivery through the Internet and special order foods for diabetics and others with health problems. Frank's Fresh Foods will change from a simple corner grocery store to a specialty food shop that provides almost person-to-person service. Frank explains to Peter that though the transition might be a bit rocky, there is a good chance that they will become even more profitable than they are at the present.

This is leadership. Leaders find a way to direct their organizations forward in a positive direction despite the adversities. They accept challenges. They are not reluctant to change. In fact, true leaders never stop thinking about change. Perhaps in our shop scenario, Frank already anticipated that a larger competitor would soon open up nearby and he already conducted a market research and developed a plan to move in the new direction. Leaders like this never seem to skip a beat when others are running for cover. This is why the first essential concept of leadership emphasizes the embracing of change. Leadership implies change. Once that change is instituted, management takes over. But do not confuse the two. Management alone, as excellent as it might be, must be focused on the "now" to be effective. Leadership looks to the future and the changes that must be made.

---

2. Any change must benefit the followers and not just the leader.

Change is psychologically difficult and individuals change only when they perceive a benefit. Any enforced change without the willingness of the followers is simply an exercise in authority—not leadership.

Peter has a problem. He is a good shop manager because he knows exactly what he is doing. He has a well-designed and smooth running store. Quite frankly, he is comfortable with the way things are presently. Now his boss, Frank, wants him to learn a whole new set of skills required for the transition to the personalized customer shop. Customers will be telling him to shop, in effect. If Peter is normal, he is not very excited about this new change.

Change is always psychologically threatening. Everyone gets comfortable in his or her own personal pattern sets. How many people get up in the morning and follow exactly the same ritual day after day? How many think of a different way to drive to work each day? And why should they? It is logical that once a way is found to do something, it is best to stick with it. Isaac Newton even noted that it was a law of nature—a body will remain at rest until it is moved by a greater force to change.

Again back to the store manager, Peter. He might initially try to talk his boss out of the change, citing the loyalty of his current customer base or minimizing the effect of the new SuperDuper Market. He might even disagree so vehemently that he feels he must leave Frank's employ. Why? Is Peter so dense he cannot see the very facts in front of him? It is doubtful. Rather, Peter is simply struggling with normal resistance to an unwelcome change.

All change is caused by a state of discomfort with the status quo. Our psychological aversion to change is so strong, that as long as we are comfortable (essentially satisfied with present conditions), we never change. Only two factors can influence a desire for change—fear of threat or prospect of gain.

If a tragedy struck Frank's Fresh Foods, say vandals entered at night and trashed the premises, then Peter might be more open to new ideas. Because the store would need to be redone in any case, it would be a good opportunity to introduce some new products or initiate some new systems such as better nighttime security. Change would be a natural process because there was a threat. The threat shattered the complacency of the status quo.

Leaders find it is much easier to lead during times of crisis because that is when the followers are most uncomfortable. They are most open to change during these times. But if a leader tries to initiate a change when individuals are comfortable, they can expect to be quite unpopular.

When Frank was trying to convince Peter that they needed to change the store, he appealed to the two factors. He noted that SuperDuper Market would undercut his customer base (fear of threat), but also noted that his business plan shows they will be even more profitable in the future (prospect of gain).

This is what leaders do. They must be change initiators. They must have one foot in the present and one foot in the future. It is easy to perceive the case of a store owner as a leader, but how about others? How exactly does a person get to be a leader, anyway?

3. The right conditions must exist to initiate a change.

Simply wanting to make a change forward is not going to make it happen. A person must be at the right place, at the right time, doing the right things with the right people to truly impact a change.

Tom Jamison was elected to the board of directors of a small Christian school in the suburban Philadelphia area, which his children were attending. He was misinformed about the time of the first meeting he was to attend and arrived late. To his surprise, the members had held an election during his absence, and because no one else wanted the position, Tom had been elected president of the board! (Tom never arrived late for another meeting in the next 15 years.) He walked into his first meeting and was given the charge to run the whole show. Despite his total inexperience and lack of knowledge, he was instrumental in leading Penn Christian Academy in Norristown, Pennsylvania, into becoming a nationally recognized preschool and primary school program.

It just as easily could not have happened. Tom could have showed up, taken a chair, and played a subordinate role without any clue that he had such tremendous leadership potential in that domain. Individuals may have latent within them extraordinary talents and abilities (their Leadership Capital), but until the conditions are right, they will not get the opportunity to display them. Leadership Conditions are primarily sociological conditions that serve as catalysts to propelling a leader into the limelight. These conditions are people, place, position, and period.

People refers to the followers of the leader. Quite frankly, if a leader has no one who will follow, he is not a leader; he is just going for a walk! Though some would argue that leaders are able to inspire and ignite followers to action, the truth of the matter is that the right chemistry between followers and leaders must preexist for this to happen.

Followers may choose not to follow for reasons such as the age of the leader, or personality, or race, or nationality, or gender. It does not matter whether these are valid; they are personal beliefs and extremely difficult to change over the short term. This explains why females have traditionally not held leadership roles outside of tolerant societies. Given the same opportunities, women can certainly perform as well and at times, even better than men. But if men never give them the opportunity, they cannot prove it.

Of course, the condition of people can be disregarded through the use of naked authority, but this should not be considered leadership. The traffic cop can direct the driver of a car to pull over, but they certainly cannot be said to be leading that driver. Leadership works only through the voluntary willingness of the followers.

Place is the domain in which the leader serves. Some individuals are very "domain-specific" in that they are only effective within one particular field or area. Isaac Newton is an example of such. Newton single-handedly contributed more to the development of science than any other individual in history. Between the ages of 21 and 27, he discovered the three laws of motion and the law of universal gravitation, made fundamental contributions to the fields of optics and light, and also developed differential calculus. His work laid the foundation for the scientific community for the next two hundred years!

Yet Newton was marginal, at best, in everything else he did. He was undistinguished as a professor, had numerous rows over petty disagreements when he served as President of the Royal Society, and spent many years of his life developing absurd ideas in biblical theology and prophesy. Nothing illustrates Newton's weaknesses outside of the science realm better than his one-year term as a member of the British Parliament.

At the age of 46, he was elected as an MP for Cambridge University, and the British Empire must have been thrilled at the thought of the greatest mind of the time sitting in the House of Commons and giving insight on the weighty issues of the day. But months went by and Newton never uttered a sound. After nearly a year had gone by in his position, he finally raised his hand and asked to speak. The chamber hushed as it waited for the eminent scientist to utter his first official words—they turned out to be a request for a window to be opened because it was stuffy inside! History records that these were the only words Isaac Newton ever uttered as a Member of Parliament.

Here is a case of a man who was brilliant in the domain of science but almost totally helpless in any other. Newton could not transfer his skills adequately from one place to the other. Some leaders are able to make the leadership transfer, such as a general becoming an elected official or a successful salesman becoming a sales manager, but there are many others who cannot.

For a leader to effectively lead, there must be a proper "fit." It is not unlike an actor finding the right role to play, or a musician discovering a piece of music that he or she can perform more masterfully than any other. Some leaders, just like actors and musicians, have a larger range and can fit in many different "places" whereas others best specialize in one domain.

Position refers to the authority of the leader. If individuals never are in a place where they can assume responsibility, they can never become leaders. This is like the example of Tom Jamison. Once he was given the positional power, he could effectively lead the school forward. In the case of the imaginary shop, Frank also was ideally positioned to make the changes he desired because he was the owner of the store.

In every organization, there are those who manage the processes and direction of the organization and those who have the capability to make decisions that would change them. Not everyone seeks to command, because with it comes more responsibility. Yet for leaders, this is where they feel they can truly demonstrate their talents and abilities. They can make a difference.

An individual who takes a position by force, such as a dictator, is seeking to usurp the leadership conditions. It does not work. The evidence from history is unmistakable. Authoritarianism demands that heavy control measures must follow. This is not only true in countries but in businesses as well. A person who has stabbed others in the back to rise to the top must watch his or her own back very closely.

Only when a position is given or earned does the individual have moral authority to lead. In contrast, when a position is taken, the person is in a position to control people—but not lead them.

Finally, the **period** of the leader refers to the time in which they serve. The times may be very favorable or very unfavorable to the parameters of the change they wish to initiate. In 1970, the shadow education minister for the out-of-power Conservative Party in the United Kingdom remarked, "No woman in my time will be prime minister or chancellor or foreign secretary." That woman was Margaret Thatcher. Yet less than a decade later, this same woman would become the first female Prime Minister in the history of her country. A lot had changed in ten years!

Period refers to all the various societal factors that impact upon an organization and the person leading it. This is one of the big arguments against the best practices approach; these practices seem to have a limited shelf life. George C. Parker, assistant dean of the Stanford Graduate School of Business, notes that managing during times of growth and prosperity demands different skills than leading during hard times. "Some leaders find it possible to adjust their styles, others do not," notes Parker. "That's why there is so much turnover at the top as we move through the normal business cycle—especially in industries where the cycle operates with a vengeance."[1]

Sometimes individuals are simply ahead of their time. Herman Melville wrote his novel *Moby Dick* in 1851. The book was largely ignored in his day and virtually forgotten until the 1930s when literary experts rediscovered and reexamined the novel. Since that time, it has been generally considered one of the greatest works of literature ever written. Melville was before his time. He was not recognized for his genius in the time and society in which he lived.

Others may possess certain values that are not appreciated at that particular juncture. Values do change. (In 1901, the dictionary definition for *uranium* read, "a worthless white metal, not found in the USA.") Discretion and integrity were not highly appreciated in leaders during the red-hot DotCom days of the 1990s, yet after corporate scandals such as Enron and WorldCom, they are valued now.

Leadership conditions determine who gets to lead and who does not. If an individual wants to direct his or her organization or group forward in a new direction, they need to be *in the right place at the right time, with the right people doing the right things.*

Another way of stating this is that before individuals will be given the opportunity to lead, they must find the place where they can hold sway, be in the period of time that is appropriate for change, hold a position that conveys authority to make change, and have people who are ready and willing to follow in that direction.

---

4. Success in leading depends on a leader's "Capital."

Once given an opportunity to lead, success will depend on the six core elements that have been effectively developed within the leader, known as his or her "Leadership Capital."

Leadership can be compared to a sports contest like soccer (European football). Imagine that I have tremendous talent as a soccer player. I might, perhaps, even be the best soccer player who has ever lived (this takes some imagination, but bear with me on the analogy). But unless I have a team (people), in which I have an active role (position), with an opponent playing against us (period), in an athletic contest of some magnitude (place); my skills will never be noticed. The skills I possess will represent my athletic capital: my potential, my assets that are waiting to be used in the right venue.

The two necessary ingredients of leadership are termed *Leadership Capital* and *Leadership Conditions*. Leadership Capital is the characteristics and talent that enables an individual to effectively lead others. It is the raw elements, the innate talents and abilities that are available to an individual. Leadership Conditions are the circumstances that permit an individual to lead others.

The use of the word *capital* is significant. *Capital* usually refers to financial resources, and in recent years has also been applied to intellectual areas. The word *capital* implies a resource that must be invested to be fully utilized and also one that can be developed and grown. In the same way, Leadership Capital is dormant until it is ignited by Leadership Conditions. These conditions are the catalysts that provide the circumstances for the individual to actually function as a leader.

Both elements, the capital and the conditions, are necessary for true leadership to take place. As a crude example, an investigator researching a crime of murder may have a suspect who he knows is capable of committing the deed. But the suspect must have had a motive, an opportunity, and the means in order to be found guilty of the crime. Just having "criminal capital," so to speak, is not enough. The conditions must all be met or the criminal could not have done what he has been accused of doing.

Leadership Conditions give an opportunity to lead; yet they are not a filter. Anyone finding him or herself with the opportunity will be either a good leader or a bad one, depending on his or her capacity to lead. This capacity is demonstrated in six key areas: vision, values, wisdom, courage, trust, and voice. These six competencies form the heart of the Ideal Leadership Model, so they must be closely examined.

Philosophical Characteristics = Vision + Values

The ideology or philosophical approach of the leader is determined by his or her **vision** and **values**. Vision can be thought of as the destination that the leader wishes to move the organization to, and values are the road that will be used to get there.

They are married together. A good vision, such as rebuilding Germany after the First World War, was completely marred by Adolph Hitler's values of race purity and hatred of Jews.

There is a verse in the Book of Proverbs in the Bible that states, *"Where there is no vision, the people perish"* (Prov. 29:18 KJV). The actual Hebrew word used for "perish" means "going off in all directions." That is an apt description of the importance of vision. Without a governing vision, a leader is living only in the here and now. He is responding and reacting, but in no way leading his followers.

Values are also critical to the leader. G.K. Chesterton said, "If I did not believe in God, I should still want my doctor, my lawyer and my banker to do so." Those transcendent values enrich and ennoble our lives. Without them, we are no better than animals.

Essentially, then, both vision and values form the philosophical base within the individual. Philosophy seeks to answer the essential questions of life: who are we, why are we here, what is real, what is the meaning of life.

Individuals with a clearly defined philosophical outlook have a clear perspective on who they are, where they are going, and what is important to them in their life. In the absence of a governing philosophy, an individual will simply melt into the faceless crowd, blending in and not making trouble.

Such individuals cannot be leaders. Leaders are out in front, which means they must have an operating philosophy that will serve them when they must make a stand *against* the popular opinion of the masses. The strength of the commitment to an individual's philosophical framework determines the strength the leader will have in times of crisis and conflict.

The philosophy of leaders, their guiding vision and governing values, will serve as a reference point to the operation of their personal and interpersonal virtues.

Personal Characteristics = Wisdom + Courage

The personal characteristics of Leadership Capital are very simple. A leader must have the **wisdom** to know what to do and the **courage** to carry it out. It is that simple. The endless surveys conducted regarding characteristics of admired leaders list the same words again and again: honest, competent, intelligent, imaginative, mature, determined, courageous, etc. Boil all these attributes down to their essence and what qualities do they describe? Wisdom and courage.

To be wise is more than just intelligent. David Halberstam's marvelous book, *The Best and the Brightest*, analyzes how the brain trust of the Kennedy administration could have blundered so badly in getting caught in the Vietnam quagmire. John F. Kennedy probably collected some of the best minds in one administration since the days of the Founding Fathers. They were brilliant men, but they lacked wisdom. Some of the most fundamental laws of military engagement were disregarded, and the consequences were devastating.[2]

Thomas Edison is credited with over one thousand discoveries. However, his first invention, the electric vote-recorder, was rejected because the company he showed it to could not see any practical use for it. His career as an inventor could have ended abruptly. Edison knew that he needed more than just theoretical knowledge. He needed to be practical; in fact, the more practical he became, the more successful he became.

But the truth of the matter is that only a fraction of those many inventions actually came from Thomas Edison himself. He had the wisdom to know that the best way to innovate was to collect the best inventors in the world and put them together under one roof. He even built a village, Menlo Park, where everyone could live. In this environment, discovery became commonplace. Out of this venture developed the company General Electric, which is today one of the world's most successful enterprises.

Great leaders are wise. They fight only the battles they know they can win, or at least are worth fighting! They make decisions that will produce the maximum benefit for the most people. They can see past problems and envision creative solutions. Wisdom is the first and most important part of leadership.

At the same time, wisdom alone does not do it. Too many have missed their window of opportunity because they hesitated. Too many have waited for others to take the risks, thinking that they can then take over when it is safe. A group of friends wrote to the missionary Dr. David Livingstone informing him that they had other men ready to join him on the mission field in Africa as soon as there was a good road to his area. Livingstone wrote back, "If you have men who will only come if they know there is a good road, I don't want them. I want men who will come if there is no road at all."

In the *22 Immutable Laws of Marketing*, Al Rias and Jack Trout demonstrate the relationship in business between courage and leadership. It requires courage to be a market pioneer because the risk of failure is very high. But those businesses that were courageous to get their products out first—Xerox in copiers, Hewlett-Packard in laser printers, Hertz in rent-a-cars—all became the market leaders. Courage is essential to leadership.

Wisdom joined with courage becomes a powerful combination. Henry Van Dyke wrote, "Genius is talent set on fire by courage." Creativity is as much an exercise in courage as it is in cognitive processing. Courage is a willingness to take risks, but these are also calculated risks, careful risks, risks that will produce the most good. Nothing is worse than a meaningless sacrifice. Courage combined with wisdom is energizing, ennobling, elevating; it is what we most admire in a leader. It is humanity at its best.

Interpersonal Characteristics = Trust + Voice

The interpersonal traits of the leader, meaning how they relate to others, are **trust** and **voice**. As with the other pairs, these two also have an interdependency.

The basic ingredient to all human relationships is trust. The reason why we can communicate, teach, trade, or conduct any interaction whatsoever between people is because of trust. Picture a person on the street asking directions. Does he follow the instructions given to them? Only if they feel they can trust the person sharing the information.

The same is true in education. The reason a person accepts the content of the lesson is based on the amount of trust the student has in the teacher.

It therefore follows that trust is foundational to leadership. No one will follow someone whom they cannot trust. An example of a breakdown in trust took place in the American Civil War. Basic military strategy at that time was to mass troops and hurl them against each other. The Union army generals, being the aggressors, usually had to attack well-entrenched Confederate army positions. The result was a tremendous loss of life. Battle-weary Union veterans began to question the wisdom of this strategy. After a series of defeats, they eventually just quit. During the Battle of Cold Harbor, the commanders gave the orders to attack and no one moved. These were seasoned soldiers who knew the consequences of their actions, but they had completely lost trust in their superiors. They just were not going to follow anymore.

The authority of the leader is based on trust. Most individuals will initially give their leaders the "benefit of the doubt." Followers realize they do not know all the facts and they must exert a certain element of blind trust, trust that is based solely on faith. But if a leader violates that trust—abuses their power, acts inconsistently, openly lies, or other such actions—they lose their authority to lead. Not coincidentally, it is when a leader loses his "trust authority" that he often reverts to "mandated authority." The only way a leader can lead without trustworthiness is through brute power. This is why Warren Bennis and Burt Nanus have written, *"The accumulation of trust is a measure of the legitimacy of leadership."*[3]

The second interpersonal characteristic—the competency of voice—is more than just the ability to speak or write well. Those with this leadership quality embody their message and know the right thing to say at the right time in the right way to the right people.

Every leader has developed the ability to transmit the force of their ideas to others. It might be through speaking (Winston Churchill and Martin Luther King), through writing (Darwin, Marx), through their example (Gandhi, Mother Theresa of Calcutta), or through the practice of their particular genius (Picasso, Einstein, Frank Lloyd Wright). In specifically writing about dissent, the Harvard political economist Albert O. Hirschman used the most compact terminology in calling this dynamic—voice.[4] Voice as a leadership competency is more than just speaking; it is exerting all possible influence over others.

Cognitive psychologists have discovered that knowledge we store in our brains is for functional use; it is structured not to satisfy an elegantly designed logical scheme, but to facilitate our daily use. This knowledge is encoded in what are termed "stories." Virtually all human knowledge is based on stories constructed around past experiences, and new experiences are interpreted in terms of old stories. Howard Gardner, in his book, *Leading Minds*, stated that every true leader has one dominant story. By that, he meant that they had one principle idea that they stood for and articulated through their life and work.[5]

Every good leader does this in some way or another. They have an overall key concept that is central to their vision, which they make a focal point of their communication. Tom Watson, for many years CEO for the IBM Corporation, posted a huge sign on the wall behind his desk with the single word "think."

It is not surprising that during his years IBM was known for hiring the most intelligent people in the marketplace. IBM placed everyone through a rigorous training program. Their research and development people were constantly making technological breakthroughs. As a result, IBM was the undisputed leader for decades in the computer and electronics market.

Wisdom, courage, trust and voice represent the psychological profile of the leader. Vision and values represent the philosophical perspective of the leader. All six of these factors constitute the *Leadership Capital* of an individual. They are the seed that must be planted in the ground of *Leadership Conditions*.

---

5. Success in leadership happens when conditions and capital coincide.

Success in leadership is not a matter of luck, but good preparation that coincides with an appropriate moment in time. These "Gateways of Leadership Initiative" are the strategic windows of opportunity that the effective leader uses.

Two domains where leadership can be clearly seen are athletic contests and warfare. Both the good coach and crafty commander carefully choose the moments to exploit their opponent's weaknesses and move onward to victory. This is true in every endeavor. For a change to make the desired impact, it must be initiated at the right time and in the right way.

Keys to Growth Leadership "Moments"

These critical moments could be called *Gateways of Leadership Initiative* or GOLI's (pronounced "golly") for short. A good GOLI is one where the initiated change is introduced at exactly the right time.

Bill Gates made his fortune by having an operating system ready when IBM was ready to enter into the personal computing market. It was not just a good, but a great GOLI, for the tiny upstart company Microsoft. But leadership means continually focusing on change, and today the giant Microsoft finds Apple constantly nipping at its heels with innovations like the iPod, iBook, and Mac Mini.

To recognize those strategic GOLI moments is where the "art" of leadership comes in. Good leaders draw on all of their resources, but at the same time, have an instinct that they must tap to know that a window of opportunity is open and the time to move is right now. The key is to take bold steps when boldness is demanded, as Napoleon so aptly noted, "When you are going to take Vienna, take Vienna."

6. Failure in leadership is a result of changing conditions or misapplied capital.

Failure happens, sometimes through neglect, other times through incompetence, and other times simply as a result of circumstances. In each case, the root of failure can be identified in either a weakness in Leadership Capital or a change in the Leader's Conditions.

No one is one hundred percent successful in any endeavor of life, and this certainly applies to leadership. Yet if a leader wishes to learn from these failures, it is necessary to identify the source. In each and every case, the cause is either in the conditions or capital.

As has already been noted, a Leader's Capital is carefully balanced between competencies, but it is also balanced *within* the same competency.

For example, a leader may not have enough courage, and in compensating goes too far off the scale and acts foolhardily. While distrust in a leader is damaging, blind trust to the point of never questioning anything is also unhealthy.

These extremes on each end of the scale of the six competencies are known as elements of "anti-leadership." They will not produce the result the leader desires, and in fact, will work against it. An individual whose leadership is mostly composed of anti-leader characteristics—Hitler and Stalin come to mind—could actually be called an "anti-leader." True leadership is the preserve of the good.

Yet a leader might be doing everything right and still find him or herself off the mark. This is because conditions do change. People who have followed a man for years may question if he is now too old and may become less loyal than before. The position may have some authority taken from it. Perhaps the time period is not as opportune for the leader as it was in the past.

These "misses" in leadership are known as *Failures of Leadership Initiative* or FOLI's (pronounced, "folly"). Warren Buffett, one of the greatest investors of all time, admits that his biggest mistakes were not acts of commission, but omission. He could have made a fortune buying Disney stock in the 1960s, but chose not to. The worst thing about FOLI's is that it is sometimes years later before they are clearly seen for what they are.

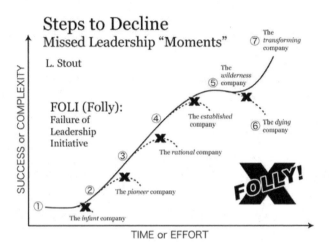

---

7. Leadership Capital is an expendable resource.

Good leaders must maintain their capital during changing conditions, which means they must practice continuous learning. Only through personal self-development can a leader continue to supply him or herself with renewable leadership energy.

In his typical direct style, John F. Kennedy summed up the attitude that leaders must maintain about personal renewal—"Leadership and learning are indispensable to one another." Note that he did not say, "*Starting to lead* and learning are indispensable to one another." Leaders must be constant 24/7 learners, but not necessarily in the formal sense. Probably no other aspect of leadership has been emphasized as much since the new millennium has begun.

- Leaders need mentors—individuals who have greater expertise and experience who can assist during difficult decision-making and problem-solving times.

- Leaders need coaches—individuals who take an interest in their overall well-being and assist in rounding out all aspects of their life in perspective to their responsibilities.

- Leaders need confidants—individuals close to them where they work who they can bounce ideas off of and suggest plans of action to get initial reactions and feedback.

- Leaders need experts—individuals who can specifically supply needed information where it is lacking in the leader's life.

The world is moving much too rapidly for anyone, and especially those seeking to lead, to go it alone.

————————————— Endnotes —————————————

1. Hamilton, Joan C. "Where's The Leadership?", *Business Week*, (9 July 2001).

2. Halberstam, David. *The Best and the Brightest* (Random House, New York, NY, 1969).

3. Bennis, Warren G. and Nanus, Burt. *Leaders: Strategies for taking charge* (HarperCollins, London, UK, 2003), 7.

4. Hirschman, Albert O. *Exit Voice and Loyalty: Responses to Decline in Firms, Organizations, and States* (Harvard University Press, Cambridge, MA, 1970).

5. Gardner, Howard. *Leading Minds: An Anatomy of Leadership* (HarperCollins, London, UK, 1996).

Key Ideas

1. The Ideal Leadership Model explains the concept of leadership—Capital within the individual activated by Conditions outside the individual.

2. The operation of leadership can be explained in seven sentences.

   - Leadership implies change and initiating change.

   - Any change must benefit the followers and not just the leader.

   - The right Conditions must exist to initiate a change.

   - Success in leading depends on a leader's "Capital."

   - Success in leadership happens when Conditions and Capital coincide.

   - Failure in leadership is a result of changing Conditions or misapplied Capital.

   - Leadership Capital is an expendable resource.

Questions for Active Leaders

1. What was the most difficult change you have had to make in leading your organization? How painful was it for the followers? Could you have done anything different to help them through the process?

2. Identify a FOLI—a missed leadership opportunity. Was it caused by poor conditions (largely outside of your control) or inappropriate capital (within your capacity to change). What did you learn from this experience?

Questions for FLOWters (Future Leaders of the World)

1. As you read through the six Leadership Capital competencies, which seem to be your natural strengths? Which do you believe might present challenges?

2. What is your best source of increasing your Leadership Capital? Do you know of possible mentors or coaches who can assist in your leadership development?

PART TWO

Leadership From A to Z
(With an Emphasis on C)

CHAPTER THREE

The First Essential—
The Necessity of Change

Little School—Big Change

Can one person make a difference? Can one individual halt the inevitable march of events and reverse them? Probably in no domain is change more difficult than in education. There are well-known cases like the educational reformer Robert Maynard Hutchins, the great University of Chicago educator, or Theodore Hesburgh who at the age of 35 became president of Notre Dame University and transformed it into one of the leading educational institutions in America. But those are major universities. Is change possible in the smallest schools?

Every year since 1979, the number of college students has decreased in the United States, which has forced the closure of hundreds of small colleges since that time. Yet a tiny junior college in New Hampshire has transformed itself in just five years into a thriving, fully accredited four-year institution. Chester College of New England is a success story where it was least expected.

The school originally was known as White Pines College, opening in 1967 with five classrooms, administrative offices, a small library, a

61

snack bar for a cafeteria, and a bookstore. The total enrollment that first year was ten students. Over the years, the school carved out a niche as an educational institution specializing in the visual arts; but by the 1990s, the financial pressures began to catch up to the school as they had with so many other small schools. The school was faced with the choice to change or die.

The Board of Trustees revised the school's mission in 1998 to offer professional arts programs guided by a strong commitment to the liberal arts and the fine arts. Four Bachelor of Arts degree programs were developed, and in 1999, the College received authorization to become a four-year baccalaureate degree-granting institution. But now came the most difficult task for the Board—who would lead the transition?

After a year-long national search, Dr. William A. Nevious was chosen as President and Chief Executive Officer of the college in December 2001. William "Butch" Nevious had an impressive academic background, to be sure, but the Board needed more than just a good educator; they needed a leader. When the search team contacted Nevious, the first thing he mentioned was his health. He had gone through surgery in May 2001 for kidney cancer and just three months later had another surgery for a gall bladder failure that shut down his remaining kidney. The interviewers were completely taken by his honesty. This man had character.

It came from a lifetime of struggle. Butch grew up in an orphanage, served in Vietnam, and struggled with a number of jobs until finally finding his niche as a photographer, gaining as much education as he could along the way. He had worked his way up at various schools throughout the United States from assistant professor to associate professor to vice president for academic affairs and finally as president of Reinhardt College in Wisconsin.

Jean Servello, one of the White Pines' administrators noted, "He knew exactly what he wanted to do with our college. You don't get sidetracked with him. The minute you get sidetracked, he whips in and makes a decision."[1]

Dr. Nevious supervised the transition to a four-year, baccalaureate degree-granting institution, stabilizing the college's financial situation, completing a multimillion dollar residence hall, tripling the number of full-time faculty members, and breaking all enrollment records in the process. In addition, the school received a ten-year accreditation from the New England Association of Schools and Colleges, significantly enhancing the college's academic standards as a four-year institution.

What was Dr. Nevious' secret? More than anything else, he was driven by the necessity of change. He knew that little White Pines Junior College, with a little over 100 students in a two-year program, was a dinosaur. He clearly saw the vision of a new institution, Chester College of New England, and focused all the resources and energies of his staff on that new objective. It worked.

This is leadership. Leaders...lead. They are out front. They point the way to a new vision, a new hope, in such a way that followers desire to go in that direction. As Colin Powell put it so well, "A good leader is someone whose people will follow him or her, if only out of curiosity."

It is difficult to envision a world without leaders. Everyone admires leaders. They teach us, they inspire us, they show us the way ahead. Leaders make us feel safe and secure during times of crisis. They make us surprised in ourselves because they make us give more of ourselves. Leaders make a difference in any government, organization, institution, club, family, and home.

Napoleon was not far off when he said he would rather have an army of rabbits led by a lion than an army of lions led by a rabbit. In almost every case, the difference between success and failure in business and commerce, education and the arts, government and diplomacy, athletics and entertainment, is trustworthy, visible, visionary, wise, courageous, and principled leadership.

Management Versus Leadership

Leaders are change-makers. Managers, on the other hand, are those who maintain the status quo. Some individuals who have been excellent as managers are simply unable to make the transition to leadership. George H.W. Bush, successor as president to Ronald Reagan, is an example of this type. He was called Mr. Resume because he had served in so many roles: U.S. congressman, UN ambassador, CIA director, and Vice President of the United States.

Many assumed that with such a broad portfolio of experience, he would make an excellent president.

But as John Podhoretz noted, "Bush is one of the finest human beings to serve in the White House—a man of infinite personal grace and dignity, loved and admired....But he was a disaster as a president and as a party leader because he was consumed by process....He did not seek to advance his ideas, or any ideas, for that matter."[2]

One reason why true leadership is so rare is because management, leadership's little brother, is so highly valued. Examine the curriculum of any MBA program and the list contains courses in *management*: operations management, marketing management, project management, production management, human resource management, financial management, and of course, strategic management. The goal in each of these courses is to find the right formula that can be plugged in when needed to keep the systems and processes of the operation running smoothly.

Management is a skill that takes years to master, and as was noted in the last chapter, no organization lasts long that does not have competent managers. To supply any product or service in a timely and cost-effective manner that meets the demands of the market requires a steady hand and solid structure. And the market rewards those who do it well with market share and organizational stability. Thank God for good managers!

Yet managers need their "big brother's" help. Management presupposes a status quo situation. Unfortunately, the world we live in never stops moving and changing. In fact, the very success of the company invites competitors who seek to find a way to produce the same products or service faster, cheaper, or better.

Quite frankly, survival in the new millennium depends on not just staying ahead of the competition, but clearly differentiating from them. Jonas Riddestrale, professor at the Stockholm School of Economics and coauthor of the popular book, *Funky Business*, notes that in the new economy, a company needs a "recipe" or idea that provides a temporary monopoly due to its innovation in packaging, marketing, function, etc.[3]

Creation of a temporary monopoly does not happen by accident. An astute leader must carefully anticipate the market's needs and expectations, and have available the product or service at precisely the time it is desired.

And as Riddestrale notes, the key is constant innovation. This is *not* what managers traditionally do. It is exactly this paradox that keeps CEOs up at night—literally!

> The thing that wakes me up in the middle of the night is not what might happen to the economy or what our competitors might do next; it is worrying about whether we have *the leadership capacity and talent* to implement the new and more complex global strategies.

> David Whitwam, former chairman/president/CEO of Whirlpool Corporation, *Leadership* is the biggest single constraint to growth at Johnson & Johnson, and it is the most critical business issue we face.

> Ralph Larsen, former chairman of the board of Johnson and Johnson, *Weak leadership* condemns an organization to death.

> *Don Blohowiak*, noted author and management expert

World of the Future

Because leaders are to have one foot in tomorrow, it would be worthwhile to stop and examine what that future world might look like. In what ways should a person who wishes to lead in tomorrow's society best prepare for what is to come?

To imagine the world of the future, it might be useful to take a quick glance at the past. Fifteen years ago the world looked drastically different than it does today. The Soviet Union was still in existence, Michael Jordon had yet to win an NBA basketball championship, and portable phones were the size of small refrigerators. Only geeks owned computers, and communication between computers was a subscriber service available to very few.

When my family and I moved to Latvia in January 1991, the contrast between the USA and the USSR made us feel like we had landed on a distant planet. In a planned economy, such as the Soviet Union had at the time, many ideas like customer service and market demand were totally alien concepts. Shops were constantly empty; and when some merchandise was available, it was very tricky to buy it. Often an item was simply on display, meaning it could not be purchased. When an item could be bought, the price was unclear and calculations were done using an abacus. Needless to say, we experienced endless confusion when it came to the routine task of buying items we needed.

But with the advent of democracy and a free-market system in August 1991, everything began to change—and that is not an exaggeration. In business, commerce, the arts, politics, education, public works, from matters major and minor ranging from renaming streets to establishing new grading systems in schools—*everything* changed. The transition was so complete that today visitors to the capital city of Riga do not feel any different than they would in any other major European city.

The fact that citizens in Eastern Europe and the former Soviet Union have had to keep abreast of change much faster than their Western counterparts might be an indicator that more leaders may emerge from this part of Europe than the Western part. They have a savvy that comes from years of coping with rapid change.

So, looking ahead 15 years in the future to the year 2020, how might a writer be describing life in the world? Patrick Dixon, one of the most renowned writers and lecturers on the future, has developed six key ingredients of the coming age based on an acronym from the word FUTURE. His six factors are Fast, Urban, Tribal, Universal, Radical, and Ethical.[4] It is hard to argue with those, and he certainly has gathered a wealth of information to support them.[5]

Rather than simply repeat Dr. Dixon's excellent points, perhaps another set of six characteristics can be offered with the same acronym. These would be Fantastic, Unusual, Timely, Unexpected, Relational, and Everything.

The future will be *fantastic*.

Who would have imagined ten years ago that practically every third-grader would own a cell phone, encyclopedias would be obsolete as entire libraries would be available digitally on-line, or that Middle-Eastern countries would be having multiparty democratic elections? So is it anymore fantastic to imagine a refrigerator that automatically orders resupplies of staple items as a standard feature? Or a Dick Tracy-type watch that serves as a telephone, camera, computer, satellite tracking device, and who knows what else?

Whatever lies in the future, it would seem totally fantastic to us right now. The 2002 film *Minority Report* starring Tom Cruise was set in the year 2054. In the film, billboards personally address customers walking by because the boards "recognize" people by their eye retina print. The police use personal jet packs for transport. Regular cars are auto programmed and drive on their own. Tiny computer spiders enter a building to conduct searches. As fantastic as it sounds, the director, Steven Spielberg, has stated that he wanted to use only those futuristic elements that are currently being researched right now. In other words, all of those science-fiction devices are on the drawing board today!

Another factor in the fantastic future is that leisure will be much more important than it is today. Because our threshold of reality is being pushed further and further out, the demands of entertainment will also be expanded. I can remember in the mid-1970s how excited I was to see an electronic ball bouncing from one side of my television screen to another. In this day and age, any child over three years of age would be bored in seconds at a game like Pong.

Today's games, be they the extreme sport variety or virtual ones using XBox or PlayStation, will get more real and require more intensity on the part of the participants. Tomorrow's generation will be donning helmets that will place them in a virtual world that will not seem that different from the real one. Why go to a golf course when it is possible to play a quick nine holes right at home? Want to visit Hawaii? Or the moon? In the future, our leisure will have no limits.

How does a person prepare himself or herself for the fantastic future? Even more important, what can a leader or an aspiring leader do to be prepared for these changes just over the horizon? In a bit of irony, the past is probably the best guide.

First, keep an open mind. Those who missed the most important innovations were those who simply could not imagine them. This is why almost all true leaders have some sense of dreaming in them. Walt Disney is an excellent example. He pioneered nearly every creative innovation in animated visual arts, and his biggest advantage was that he was not afraid to dream. Cartoons were immensely popular as previews before motion pictures in the early part of the 20th century, but Disney asked, why can't there be a full-length animated cartoon? It seemed fantastic to everyone in the motion picture business because it had never been done before. The experts doubted that anyone would want to sit through an hour-and-a-half cartoon; they questioned the strain on people's eyes; but they also believed that it was technically not possible.

Disney had in mind adapting a Grimm's fairy tale of Snow White because it had all the elements of a great story (sympathetic dwarfs, evil queen for the heavy, prince and girl for romance). But there were innumerable obstacles to overcome. He had to develop new animation techniques involving larger painted cels and drawing boards as well as photographic techniques to create the illusion of depth. Because no one besides him knew how to do this, he had to hold training classes for his artists three nights a week. Added to all of that was music to be coordinated with the action. The costs were astronomical for their time and *Snow White* was nicknamed "Disney's Folly" because no one imagined it would work.

No one but Walt Disney, that is. When the first full-length animated film was released in color and sound in 1937, the critics were not just silenced, they were moved to tears. For the film's remarkable achievement, Walt Disney was awarded with an Honorary Oscar—the film was "recognized as a significant screen innovation which has charmed millions and pioneered a great new entertainment field for the motion picture cartoon." Amazingly, *Snow White* has continued to this day to make money for the Disney Corporation!

Keeping an open mind does not mean a total lack of discernment or discretion. An open mind must also be balanced with practical reasoning. IBM designed a keyboard that operated by infrared and needed no connecting cords attaching it to the computer. It never took off because the consumers did not have a reason to use their keyboards at any distance from the monitor. It was a nice feature that the engineers dreamed up, but who needed it?

In the fantastic future, the question must be asked *should* it be done, not simply *can* it be done. As we will see when we look at technological advances, these questions need to be asked loudly.

The future will be *unusual*.

Life was much simpler a generation ago. In the United States, there were three major television networks, three brands of automobiles, and three major airlines, but usually two major brands of everything else: rental cars, national newspapers, soft drinks, athletic shoes, cameras, cereals, toothpaste, credit cards, and so on. There was only one mail delivery service and one telephone company, which offered one type of home phone (big, black, and heavy).

Today we live in a personalized society. Everyone wants to be unique. Just stop and look at the proliferation of product offerings. Seiko offers 5,000 different models of watches. Nokia has 3,000 varieties of covers for their phones. The Disney Corporation offers a new product every single day! Dell simply offered consumers a chance to customize the design of their computers, and they became a global giant almost overnight.

In the future, if it is not unusual, it simply will not be noticed. Even church leaders know this to be true. When Robert Schuller accepted a call from the Reformed Church in America to go to Garden Grove, California and start a new church in the mid-1950s, the only place available for services was an old drive-in movie theater. The novelty of the country's first "walk-in/drive-in" church attracted people from all over Orange County, and after six years Schuller had grown a sizeable congregation of over 1,000 members. The decision was made to finally build a sanctuary.

When the architect produced the plans, they looked like a standard church building. But Schuller knew that to keep the uniqueness they had already established, they could not go backwards. He was a man with an eye on the future. He conceived the idea of an indoor Garden of

Eden—a church of glass—and the Crystal Cathedral was born. The Crystal Cathedral in Garden Grove, California is today home for more than 10,000 members and seen around the world on television by millions more.

The leader of the future will need to cope with this constant quest for the unusual. It will require a resistance to a one-size-fits-all approach to anything. Not only will consumers require a unique product or service, the workers themselves also will be seeking a "personalized" approach, which will mean customized benefits, workplace, and schedules.

Stop and think about this for a moment. If automation takes over, what exactly is left? We will still need car mechanics, someone needs to be around to turn on the machine in the factory, and seeing a doctor will still need to be done in person—but the list of personalized activities is shrinking every day. More and more, routine activities involving shopping to banking to entertainment can be done from home and on-line.

For example, what might a bank manager do in the future? Since most transactions will be handled electronically, these can be done with workers who can be located anywhere. In fact, an exceptionally good loan processor might work for more than one company at a time. The old days when the manager could do MBWA, Management By Walking Around, are rapidly disappearing. The manager of tomorrow will need to be like a personalized management consultant—tailoring work assignments around the particular specialists who can best perform them, then design the best compensation package available to that specialist to keep them on the job.

Yet at the same time, there will also be a need to maintain some solid standards in the midst of this swirl of here-today-gone-tomorrow. The demands of the "unusual" society will shift the focus more and more to values. Peter Drucker, the famous management expert, notes, "In the next society, the biggest challenge for the large company, especially for the multinational—may be its social legitimacy, its values, its mission, its vision. Increasingly, in the next society's corporation, top management will, in fact, be the company. Everything else will be outsourced."[6]

Core values such as integrity, excellence, social responsibility, safety, and security, all provide a stable base regardless of an individual's personal preferences. Leaders who demonstrate these values will be highly valued themselves.

The future will be *timely*.

One of the great absolutes of life is that no one gets more time than anyone else. We all are awarded 168 hours a week; no one gets more and no one gets less. However, the quest has always been to pack more and more activity into those hours. The desire has been that by saving time, we are more productive. The key to this productivity is technology, and the future has been continually pushing the envelope to shrink the time necessary for any and every activity.

Consider the simple act of shopping. While for most men, this is about as pleasurable as an appointment with a dentist, for the female of the species, shopping produces great enjoyment. Typically, a visit to a shop means a leisurely browse through the aisles looking at the variety of products, asking the clerks about specific product specifications or availability, and then going through a checkout to make the purchases. In the future, this scenario will seem as outdated as a one-room schoolhouse.

First, even going to a store is becoming more and more unnecessary. There is hardly any item that cannot be purchased on-line today. Buying and selling has become so routine through the Internet, that as of June, 2006, over 1.2 million Americans rely on their eBay businesses for their primary or secondary income.[7] This will only continue to grow in the future, especially as consumer confidence grows. The option of choosing from an almost endless assortment of product offerings coincides with the "unusual" aspect of the future mentioned previously.

Surely some people will still want to actually see and touch the product, won't they? Of course, but the shop in the future will be very different. Instead of bar codes on products, they will have RFIDs, Radio Frequency Identification Devices. These are pinhead size devices that produce radio bar codes. Because they are so extremely tiny, they can be attached to any product. Once these are in full-scale use, shopping will never be the same. A customer will simply pick up the items they want and walk out the door—the price will be automatically registered and the price deducted from the customer's credit card or bank account. Shoplifting (and the cost passed on to consumers as a result of it) will be eliminated. Inventories of stocks will be constantly and completely accurately maintained. When an item is sold out at one store, it could be instantly tracked in another.

RFIDs will be able to remind consumers when a product life cycle is nearing an end, so that the annoying "burnout" need never happen. Lost articles will be able to be instantly found (probably in a neighbor's house). All of this will help the man and woman of the future save time—and the future will be extremely time conscious.

The speed of technology is directly dependent to the speed of computers. One barometer that has been a fairly reliable guide to the progress in computing speed has been Moore's Law, which states that the speed of computers will double every 18 months. If that holds up, computers in the year 2020 will be ten times faster than they are today, which assumes using present silicon chip technology. There is technology being developed that promises to deliver computer power that is *thousands* of times faster than today! When this arrives, the speed of everything we do will exponentially increase.

Already the vast power available to the average man is awesome. One change that this has manifested already is less manpower intensive activity. My son Aaron is an aspiring filmmaker, and he has noted that with his Mac iBook, digital movie camera, and appropriate software, he is able to produce a better film by himself than a studio with hundreds of employees were capable of a generation ago.

The leader of tomorrow must understand that the future will be technologically driven in the pursuit of quicker, faster, and better. Is this necessarily a good thing? Every leader of the future will be forced to deal with much more serious ethical issues than those faced today.

The questions of privacy, security, and when technology becomes "technopoly" (Neil Postman's term) will not just be academic discussions at conferences but the real stuff of the everyday world.[8] This is a major consideration in the field of RFIDs, for example. Once these are attached to a product, they can be tracked anywhere. Those who are concerned already about the level of intrusion brought about by market researchers who track personal consumer habits will have their hands full with these little guys telling anyone with a listening device exactly what we have in our possession.

The leader of the future faces a disturbing paradox, best expressed by University of Cambridge professor Ian Wilson, "However good our futures research may be, we shall never be able to escape from the ultimate dilemma that, all our knowledge is about the past, and all our decisions are about the future."

The future will be *unexpected*.

The new millennium has already had many unpleasant surprises: terrorist attacks in America, Madrid, Bali, Beslan, Moscow, and London to name just a few; a tsunami that caused unbelievable devastation in the Indian Ocean region; major hurricanes in the Gulf of Mexico causing massive destruction; and a strange new disease that appeared out of China.

SARS (Severe Acute Respiratory Syndrome) emerged in mid-November 2002 in Guangdong Province, China. This initial outbreak involved a population that handled wildlife and livestock. With an estimated incubation period lasting less than 14 days, the virus spread with surprising speed and soon infected approximately 1,290 people with 55 reported deaths in Mainland China alone. The virus began to spread and within a short while, 27 countries on six continents began to report illnesses from it.

If there is one certainty of what can be expected of the future, it is the unexpected. No matter how effective our forecasting models or scenario planning, fate is going to throw us things we never imagined.

Even major events catch the experts by surprise. When the Berlin Wall came down in November 1989, I went back and researched if any major newspaper or magazine columnist had foreseen that event in their predictions for the new year. I could not find a single one that even hinted of such a result, even given Mikhail Gorbachev's policies of *glasnost* and *perestroika*, which should have alerted some analyst that ramifications should be expected.

So how can the leader of the future expect the unexpected? Noted author Jim Collins tells a fascinating story of a group of management experts who assembled in 1998 to discuss what the world would look like in 2050. As the group was discussing the various science fiction scenarios, Collins came up with another approach. He asked the group to envision a similar group to theirs sitting in a room 50 years in the future and shaking their heads at what is presently held to be truths about the world. "Putting it another way, I asked this: 'What do we, today, take for granted, that in just 50 years our successors sitting in this same room, will marvel that we actually believed to be true?'"

Collins himself could not imagine that his question itself contained an unimaginable consequence. That meeting was held on the top floors of one of the towers of the World Trade Center in New York City.[9]

Leaders who are serious about planning for the future have to be extremely critical of their assumptions and prejudices. We no longer believe that it is risk-free to hold a meeting. We understand the hazards associated with international travel. We know that a world crisis can break at any moment.

To expect the unexpected means being reasonably prepared for any and all eventualities. Business schools in the future will teach crisis management as an integral part of their curriculum. Even small businesses and organizations will have contingency plans. Expect it to happen!

The future will be *relational*.

Dr. Danica Purg, founder and director of the IEDC Bled School of Management, is one of Europe's leading educators. She has studied at some of the finest institutions in the world, has founded a major university as well as CEEMAN (Central and East European Management Development Association), which has members from 39 countries in Europe, North America, Africa, and Asia. She has received numerous honorary degrees and other recognitions throughout Europe and Russia. Yet when Dr. Purg was asked at a conference what she considered her greatest accomplishment in life, she stated, "Developing my network of contacts."

As the future world becomes more and more impersonal, with interactions at the shop, the bank, the supermarket, and even at work being mostly with machines rather than men, the need for human contact will accelerate. Humans are social creatures by nature, and no amount of computer interface or electronic communication will substitute for good old face-to-face, flesh-to-flesh contact.

Another reason why interpersonal interaction will be critical is because of the importance of trust. Trust is the essential element in all human endeavors, from the micro to macro-level. With all the innovations in marketing over the years, word of mouth is still the most valued form of advertising. We act based on the trust we have in others.

In the next society, there will be so many choices and so little time to make decisions, individuals will increasingly draw upon their networks to assist them. Leaders like Dr. Purg already understand and are acting this way.

However, in the future these interactions will undoubtedly be briefer and more sporadic. The astute manager must be more effective in his or her people skills. This will mean clearer and crisper conversations. This will involve more empathy and understanding for differences and perspectives. This will mean valuing every personal contact because it will be more and more rare.

The future will be *E-everything*.

In the future, everything—absolutely everything—will be touched by the integration of technology, computing, and human interaction. Consider one of the most resistant-to-change domains—education. Throughout the world, the concepts of education are fairly universal. Children from approximately age 6 to 12 receive primary education and those in their teen years are either taught a trade or are prepared for some form of higher education. Higher education can mean a particular trade taught at a junior college or technical school, or the beginning of a university degree program. An individual awarded a bachelor's degree has learned the essential elements of his or her particular specialty or major, and should they wish to continue their studies, they will seek to master it, (hence the name, Master's Degree), and if they continue to study, they will know it well enough to teach others or contribute something new to the field in which they will receive a Ph.D. (literally, Philosophy Doctorate, meaning that an individual understands the underlying philosophy and therefore can see the entire scope of it).

The underlying assumption has been that work and study are separate from one another. A person studies so that he is able to do his particular job. But more and more, it has become apparent that this strict dichotomy is not working for the rapidly changing world. If present trends continue, it will become necessary to continuously and simultaneously study *and* work.

This will require breaking away from the traditional classroom and buildings of brick and mortar. The classroom of tomorrow will be small workgroups in homes and work places, utilizing multimedia and the Internet. Already this is happening. Over 90 percent of all universities in America offer some form of distance learning with their curriculum. There are now 244 colleges and universities that offer degrees completely on-line. The University of Phoenix, for example, has 240,180 students enrolled for on-line studies, making it by far the largest institution of higher learning in the country. These schools offer greater flexibility and variety than in-residence schools could ever hope to match.

Education in the future will be extremely flexible and tailored to the individual probably beginning right at the undergraduate level. Instead of accepting a standard curriculum, students will choose from universities throughout the world to select a unique blend of courses that suit their particular interests and career goals.

With the increasing capabilities of on-line education, some futurist experts predict that university professors will be the rock stars of tomorrow. The best teachers will be in the greatest demand, and they will be accessible to all. In-residence educational activities will be special events. The ivy-covered halls may become museums.

If this happens in education, what field will it *not* happen in? Financial services are already increasingly on-line, and there is discussion that the traditional stock trader will go the way of the ticker-tape machine. Medical breakthroughs are moving past healing of diseases and injuries and towards enhancement of human ability and potential. The list can be extended indefinitely. From trade and service, to energy, to health care, to education, to media, and entertainment—in every domain, the e-world will continue to dominate.

Leadership for the Future

So what will the leader of the future look like? Will future leadership be drastically different from what is needed for today? Given the outlook, we can make the following projections about the skills and attributes that will be valued in tomorrow's world.

Quick and Clear Communication Skills

When my children were growing up, I told them that no matter what profession they chose in life, they would have to be able to speak and write clearly if they expected to succeed. That same advice is still true for tomorrow's generation. However, what will be more valued is the ability to communicate *succinctly*. Given the increasingly rapid pace of life, individuals who will be able to concisely express their thoughts into words, in either verbal or written form, will be the ones who will be most successful.

Insightful Skills

When Latvia became an independent nation, the three fields of study that saw the greatest increase at the universities were business, foreign languages, and psychology. The first two were obviously tied to the interest in the free-market economy and globalization, but the third seemed to touch upon an interest that went much deeper. In the old Soviet system, Marxism was said to explain everything that was needed about the human condition. When the fresh air of freedom came to the Baltic nations, understanding other people was of peak interest because it was seen as a necessity to adapt to the emerging democracy.

As the future unfolds, people will adapt and change. Already children are growing up much faster than their parents ever imagined. Elderly people are studying and learning new skills. The leader of the future will have to be more astute in knowing how to relate to others. This will mean a keener sense of intuition, caring, and building of relationships. The boss who knows only how to give orders will find himself leading no one.

Ingenious Problem-Solving Skills

One futurist magazine predicts that the secretary of the future will be an "administrative response specialist" who will possess situation-management and problem-anticipation skills. Actually, the same might be said for virtually any position in the world of business and commerce.

With every business competing equally for talent and information due to globalization and the instant access provided by the Internet, the one edge is anticipating the next trend or problem and being ready for it.

Leaders who possess an imagination that is combined with sound reasoning skills will always have one foot in the future. This is far beyond strategic planning. The future leader will always have something new in mind, be it an innovation in a product or service, promoting an employee into another position, or studying a new area or subject that will be needed for the days ahead. He will never be caught flat-footed by the future.

Practical Life-Management Skills

The promotion of a balanced lifestyle has been talked about for years, but the leader of the future will find it more than just a nice idea. It will be a necessity. One constant, through all of history, is that every single person on the planet gets exactly 168 hours a week in which he or she is to live.

How those hours are used is extremely personal, but an imbalance between the number of hours devoted to work against those at home and personal well-being will take a much heavier toll in the future than they do today.

There has been a revival of interest in religion through the 1990s to today, which might be because the transience of life has awakened a need for a transcendence to cope with it. The leader of tomorrow will probably be a spiritual person. The rush from activity in either leisure or work will not provide the necessary peace and contentment that comes only with a relationship with the Almighty. By having his or her head in the clouds, so to speak, they will be able to keep both feet on the ground.

Endnotes

1. Binder, Steve, "The Path to a Presidency," *The Southern Illinoisan*, May 19, 2002.

2. Podhoretz, John. *Bush Country*: How Dubya Became A Great President---While Driving Liberals Insane (St Martin's Griffin, New York, NY, 2004).

3. Riddestrale, Jonas and Nordstrom, Kjelle. *Funky Business: Talent Makes Capital Dance* (Financial Times Management, London, UK, 2002). Quote was taken from lecture at Stockholm School of Economics in Riga in 2003.

4. Nixon, Patrick. *Futureworld: Six Faces of Global Change* (Profile Books, London, UK, 2004).

5. www.globalchange.com is one of the most complete sites on the future available.

6. Drucker, Peter, "Will the Corporation Survive" *The Economist* (November 3, 2001).

7. Creamer, Matthew, "A Million Marketers" *Advertising Age* (June 26, 2006).

8. Postman, Neil. *Technopoly: The Surrender of Culture to Technology* (Vintage Books, New York, NY, 1993).

9. Collins, Jim. "Viewpoint: Jim Collins" *Business: The Ultimate Resource* (Perseus, Cambridge, MA, 2002), 236.

Key Ideas

1. The future will be fantastic. The future leader must maintain an open mind together with practical sense.

2. The future will be unusual. The future leader must seek uniqueness with solid standards.

3. The future will be timely. The future leader must cope with the pressure for faster, smaller, better products and services.

4. The future will be unexpected. The future leader will question his or her own assumptions and develop contingencies for the unexpected.

5. The future will be relational. The future leader will carefully develop his or her network and use it judiciously.

6. The future will be E-everything. The future leader will understand that no matter what field of endeavor he or she is in, it will be rapidly changing with technological progress.

Questions for Active Leaders

1. What aspect of the FUTURE appears the most daunting? In other words, in what areas do you believe will be your greatest challenges in the future?

2. Considering the importance of being prepared for the "unusual," what practices in forecasting or scenario planning do you currently use? Are they adequate?

Questions for FLOWters (Future Leaders of the World)

1. The "relational" part of the future is crucial. What relationships are you building now that you believe will still be important 15 to 20 years from now?

2. There have been many films about the future, especially in recent years. In your opinion, which ones seem to present the most serious ethical issues to think about?

CHAPTER FOUR

The Second Essential—
The Psychology of Change

Yesterday's Goat—Today's Hero

When Jack Welch took over as CEO of GE in April 1981, he replaced Reg Jones, a leader so highly respected he had been named CEO of the decade by one leading business journal. No less, the prestigious *Wall Street Journal* had declared Jones a "management legend." The 45-year-old Welch was only the eighth CEO in the storied 121-year history of General Electric. Obviously, he had very big shoes to fill.

The safe bet would have been to maintain Jones' structure and systems. After all, GE was one of the most respected and profitable enterprises in the United States. Why mess with success? But Welch was not satisfied with the success of GE. He looked over the horizon and saw trouble. He recognized that GE had many product lines that were not competitive. He questioned if their structure was lean enough to quickly adapt to market changes. Quite simply, Jack Welch was uncomfortable with where GE was sitting in the early 1980s, and as CEO, he decided to do something about it.

The rest, as they say, is history. Welch introduced radical product line restructuring and downsizing that caused havoc to the GE company. He replaced 12 of his 14 business heads. He eliminated over 100,000 jobs. He sold off cherished GE product lines. All this activity hardly won him friends. The media nicknamed him, "Neutron Jack."

Yet when Jack Welch retired in September 2001, he was widely recognized as one of the most successful corporate executives in the history of American business. During his 20-year tenure, GE led virtually every market it entered, share prices soared, and GE outperformed 93 percent of the Fortune 500 in total return on investment in the same period of time.

Jack Welch was a leader if ever there was one. But he encountered massive resistance to his efforts because he was leading an organization that was comfortable. Welch knew if he was going to make the changes he wanted to make, he had to make people uncomfortable.

Comfortable Versus Uncomfortable

The very first psychologist, Aristotle, noted that life constantly revolves around the states of pleasure and pain. All motivation, said the great Greek philosopher, was either a pursuit of pleasure and/or an avoidance of pain. Though motivation theory today is seen as a bit more complex than that, there is something to be said for this simplistic equation.

The words *comfort* and *discomfort* perhaps describe the competing states more accurately. The state of comfort does not mean a complete satisfaction with life. Numerous surveys conducted in the United States show that a majority of workers are not happy with their jobs, yet this does not mean they are ready to leave. They stay because they are comfortable.

Comfort means that there is an acceptance of the present status. It means that a person tolerates his condition to the extent that it meets his physical demands and/or emotional well-being. Comfort is the state where the mind automatically knows what to expect; therefore, there is no thinking or planning required for what happens next.

The human brain operates by pattern sets. Anyone who has ever taken up a new sport discovers how this process works. Golf, for example, requires a complex set of physical requirements if the golfer is to have any success in hitting the ball straight down the fairway. The eyes must stay on the ball, the head must be kept down, the grip must be maintained tightly on the handle, the hips and hands must swing together congruently—and trying to remember all of this at one and the same time is almost impossible!

So the beginning golfer simply concentrates on one aspect—like keeping his or her head down while striking the ball. If the head is pulled up too soon, the ball will often slice off to the side. After many, many swings in which the head is maintained in the proper position, the golfer realizes that he or she is not thinking about it, like they were previously. They can now focus on another part of the swing.

The brain has established a pattern. It accepts that when these particular parameters are present, the head is to remain down and not jerk up. As the practice is continued, it gets to the point where the golfer is almost unable to jerk his or her head up, even if he or she wants to.

In the same way, the mind sets patterns for every aspect of life. The purpose is so the brain is free to do other, nonrepetitive tasks. Once these patterns are set, they create a "comfort" in the mind of the person that this particular issue is settled. It is like a puzzle that has been completed. There is no reason to fool with it anymore—it is done.

This helps explain why individuals with smart brains will practice behavior that they know is personally destructive. Habits such as smoking, alcohol abuse, or other addictions are not addressed because individuals simply find themselves "comfortable" in doing them.

I can use myself as an example in this regard. I have a bad habit, I admit, and it is that I use too much salt on my food. Being married to a nurse for the past three decades, I have been made fully aware of the hazards of excessive sodium in my diet. I know that it has been linked to arthritis, cardiovascular diseases, heart diseases, high blood pressure, hypertension, kidney diseases, liver diseases, ulcers, and so on, and so on.

Yet as soon as my wife's back is turned, I grab the saltshaker and load up my food with it. Why? It is simple—I like the taste of salt. I am comfortable in using it. I do not want to change, because the perceived threats are not real enough to me. In other words, the present circumstances are more real than the uncertain future scenarios.

Yet let us imagine that I go to the doctor, and she informs me that I have all the signs of emerging health problems brought on my excessive salt usage. I am told that if I do not seriously cut back on my sodium intake, I will soon end up in the hospital.

Suddenly, salt becomes my worst enemy. I throw the saltshaker away. I even check the sodium content on packages. What has changed? I still like the taste of salt, but now, I am no longer comfortable using it. I have a new reality that includes a future that is unpleasant, which I wish to avoid.

It follows logically that when this "comfort" is disturbed, it is troubling and upsetting. Discomfort is caused when the perceived comfort is found to be unacceptable, just like my salt usage.

What does this have to do with leadership? Everything! If leadership is all about change, then it follows that to move followers out of their present condition, they *must* be made to be uncomfortable. Comfortable people do not change; they have no reason to. Only uncomfortable people are changeable people.

Uncomfortable Followers Are the Only Followers

This was the problem that Jack Welch had to contend with. He realized that cherished traditions had to be abandoned if they were not helping the company become more profitable and able to cope with the future. That even meant cutting back on the sacrosanct GE Research and Development Center. Here was a company originally founded by Thomas Edison, the inventor of the modern concept of research and development. For the entire twentieth century up until 1986 (five years after Welch took over), the General Electric Company boasted more patents than any other corporation in America. GE's R&D Center, supplemented by over 100 product-oriented labs, was one of the most respected operations in the world. It boasted two Nobel Laureates. But by the time Welch retired in 2001, GE was not even ranked in the top 20 companies in research. As prestigious as it was, GE no longer needed to be at the top in research and development. That was yesterday, and Welch was building for tomorrow.

Welch understood the psychology of change. People do not change when they are comfortable. In fact, they will seriously resist it so they can remain in their comfort. Change is only possible when people are uncomfortable.

George W. Bush won his first term of office in the most closely contested election in American history. For his first nine months in office, he continued to be a president with barely 50 percent of the populace behind him. Then came 9-11, and his poll numbers went into the stratosphere. The horrors of the terrorist attacks shook Americans out of their security and now, in their state of discomfort, they were looking for a way forward.

Leaders are wanted, desired, and followed when the followers are naturally uncomfortable. It might be due to a disaster, such as 9-11, or due to other conditions that simply pose a threat to basic standards of living. No group is more intractable than labor union officials, and union leaders are constantly fighting for higher wages or increased benefits for their members. When they suddenly reverse themselves and support cutbacks, we can be assured that they do not do it out of compassion for management. They do it because they recognize that the company is under threat and their members will be out of a job unless they change their position.

Leading during times of crisis or difficulty is "easy" in the sense that followers look to the leader during these times. It is one reason why Americans have never in their long history ever voted out of office a president who chose to run during times of war. People psychologically need to know that there is someone who is delivering them from their present uncomfortable circumstances.

What are leaders to do, however, when the followers are comfortable? In effect, they are unable to lead in a different direction, and in fact, will find all efforts thwarted if they try to do so. Even if the facts are on the side of the leader—if the resistance is strong enough, he or she cannot lead. Even in scientific discovery, Thomas Kuhn (the man who gave us the term "paradigm") explained that any new theory or paradigm is initially resisted within the established scientific field because it causes a reconstruction of prior assumptions and the reevaluation of prior facts.

There is only one answer. Before leaders can lead, they must make their comfortable followers *uncomfortable*.

A leader can make followers uncomfortable through **threat of loss**.

In the imaginary scenario of the doctor visit, I was advised that the health problems associated with excessive sodium usage were no longer theory but a reality in my life. The health that I took for granted could very well be deprived from me. The thought of this took root and it became a new reality. Note that the only thing that truly changed was my perception. One minute I was happy using salt and the next minute I was not. To initiate change among followers who are complacent, leaders must be painters of a new perspective.

Researchers have found that threat of loss is a more powerful motivator than a perceived gain. By way of a very simple illustration, there is an old story of two female candy sellers working the same booth at a fair, yet one had a much longer line waiting to be served than the other. The difference was that one seller would put an excess of candy in the bag, and then remove an amount until it got to the desired weight. The other seller put in less and always had to add more to get the right amount. Even though the end result was exactly the same, customers felt somehow cheated when they saw some of their candy being removed and thus avoided this seller.

There is a whole field known as behavioral finance that studies this phenomenon. A person will be delighted over saving $10 off a $20 shirt, yet scorn saving $10 off a $200 item. Richard Thaler conducted an experiment where he told students they were to assume they had just won $30 and were then offered a coin-flip upon which they would win or lose either $9. Seventy percent of the students opted for the coin-flip. Yet when exactly the same proposition was presented as an *option* between a certain $30 or a coin flip in which they either got $21 or $39, a much smaller proportion, just 43 percent, opted for the coin-flip.

When given choices, employees are always going to weigh loss as more valuable than perceived gain. I conducted leadership training for the managers of one of the major banks in Latvia, and as a part of the session we discussed what actions among the employees were discouraged and what actions were rewarded. After some discussion, it was discovered that they were exactly the same thing! A worker who displayed initiative was commended, but only if the initiative proved successful. If it did not, there were repercussions.

The managers had been trying to figure out why their workers were not showing more initiative at their work when there were nice bonuses attached to them, but the answer suddenly became very clear. The possibility of loss after a failed initiative far outweighed the possibility of gain.

Human beings, like virtually all animals, have a very strong preservation instinct. In fact, there is an emotional center of the brain that triggers a "flight or fight" response whenever a threat is perceived. A person walking through the woods and seeing a snake strike out at them does not stand back and comment, "Oh look—a snake. This represents potential danger. I should remove myself from this area of danger by rapidly proceeding in the opposite direction in an expedient manner."

No, that is not what happens. The person instantly jumps away as the brain triggers the body into an immediate response *that happens without thinking*. The response is an automatic reflex. Threat is a powerful motivator.

This is why those in an authority position have traditionally found that threats, intimidation, and pressure are much more effective than positive motivators. As one manager put it to me quite simply, "Larry, when I yell they jump; when I bargain, they laugh."

But leaders should resist the natural tendency to gravitate toward the threat of loss to motivate a change in behavior. Yes, it works, but only to a certain degree. An individual motivated by threat of loss will move only to the point that they feel the threat is diminished—and no further. An individual motivated by gain will continue to move ahead, because continual movement promises more reward.

To again use the salt problem—I would seek to find the absolute base line that would not cause me to have health problems. I would have no motivation to go past that point. My only desire would be avoidance of a problem. It works—but there is another way.

*A leader can make followers uncomfortable through the **possibility of gain**.*

Let us imagine that the doctor gave me a different diagnosis. She told me my health was fine and that I was in no danger. However, she mentioned that since salt retains water, I could easily lose some kilograms off my weight by simply changing my diet and using less salt. She noted that I would probably have more energy, sleep better, and even enjoy better marital relations with my wife.

Now I throw away that nasty saltshaker, but not because of fear, but because I am excited about improving my health and enjoying all the benefits that will go with that. This is what leaders should strive for. They should find the "trigger" in their followers that will make them *want* to move in a new direction.

An exercise I use in my trainings on motivation with managers is to ask them to imagine that they have been approached about participating in a project that will require them to work an extra ten to fifteen hours a week for the next six to eight weeks. What incentive can they be given that will make them actually want to participate in this project?

The responses are always varied. Of course, someone quickly suggests a large financial bonus.

Others, though, consider the tax ramifications and suggest instead a paid vacation or some expensive personal item like a watch or jewelry. Still others think in more psychological terms and would like the project itself to be stimulating and exciting, and open to learning new skills. The point is, there is not one universal motivator that will work with everyone.

This represents a problem for a leader who wishes to find the possibility of gain to initiate a change in the followers' behaviors. Threat of loss is a fairly collective concern, whereas gain is not. This is yet another reason why it is not used as often as it should be among leaders.

To Change or Not to Change—That is the Question

Given all the difficulty to lead a change, it sounds almost impossible—yet it happens! It begins with a small core of initiators, as few as two or three percent of an organization. A good leader must begin by aligning him or herself with a committed group or team who are just as committed to the change. We could call these the "change makers."

There is a second tier that is readily influenced by these change makers, usually made up of about 12 to 15 percent of an organization. They are important because they will also be enthusiastic about the change, although they are not initiators. We could call these the "first followers."

The large group in the middle, generally as many as two thirds of the total, are the ones who follow simply because it is now the thing to do. We could call these the "herd followers."

The last group in an organization consists of those who never truly go along with change. They make up about 13-17 percent of the organization. They either have too much vested in the status quo or resent the change for other personal reasons. We could call these the "change resisters."

Here is a breakdown of our four groups involved in a change process:

- 2-3 percent "change makers"
- 12-15 percent "first followers"
- 65-70 percent "herd followers"
- 13-17 percent "change resisters"

Group psychologists note that any major change in the direction of an organization will break down roughly into these various groups. Obviously there are those who are strongly for the change and those who are strongly against it. Who wins?

Kurt Lewin provided a practical technique for assessing the success of a change situation known as the force-field analysis. He described change as a sort of tug-of-war between the driving forces for the change and those resisting it.

Borrowing from that concept, the first step to making a change is to identify the balance of power involved in the issue. As the above numbers show, it is important for a leader to have a good solid base to support the change process. These "change makers" and "first followers" will then cause the "herd" to follow and marginalize the "change resisters."

But just as ancient battle techniques dictated that it took three times the force of a stationary, entrenched enemy to remove it, so the leader must have a solid mass moving in the same direction if there is any hope to effect a change.

Liz Clark has outlined a very useful formula for calculating the difficulty of the change process.[1]

C = (ABD)>X

- C = Change
- A = Dissatisfaction with the status quo
- B = Desirability of the proposed change
- D = Practicality of the change (minimum risk/disruption)
- X = Cost of changing.

Keeping in mind what we said previously, when the followers are already uncomfortable, then the "A" factor and "B" factor is very high and it is easier to effect a change. However, when they are comfortable, it is apparent from the formula that virtually *all* the factors are against the one desiring to initiate a change.

The formula also notes that costs as well as people are a major factor influencing a change in an organization. But a good leader should be able to calculate the cost factor and plan for it. These are "manageable" areas. The "leadership" area comes into play in using the drivers for change to move the herd and overwhelm the resisters.

To see how this works in the real world, we will look at three major organizational changes: one that worked, one that did not, and one that is in the making. They are the Swiss watch industry, the Union of Soviet Socialist Republics, and the United States Military.

Change That Worked—The Swiss Watch Industry

The Swiss established their first full-fledged, mechanized watch factory in 1839, and for the next 150 years were the undisputed leader in watch manufacturing. Since the 1920s, watchmaking was one of the most important and lucrative industries in Switzerland. In 1931, several smaller watchmakers banded together under one holding company,

ASUAG, in an attempt to deal with the worldwide depression. Three years later, the Swiss government became an investor in ASUAG, and provided enough capital to buy into other leading watch manufacturers. Each member of ASUAG continued to operate independently, but the Swiss government regulated permits to manufacture and export whole watches, movements, or individual components in an attempt to protect the reputation of the Swiss-made label.

By 1970, there were 1620 Swiss watch companies employing 89,000 people. In 1974, the Swiss produced 88.8 million watches, all but 4.4 million for export. This accounted for 43 percent of the world market (by volume) in watches. Yet there was trouble on the horizon, and ironically, the Swiss produced it themselves.

It was quartz technology. In 1967, the first quartz wristwatch was introduced by the Swiss Horological Electronic Center, a group founded by a number of Swiss firms that had pooled their resources to develop the new oscillating quartz watch. These were incredibly accurate, and could display either a digital or analog time.

But the rest of the Swiss industry thought of this as a passing fad, and by the mid-1970s, more than half of the watches produced in Switzerland were still mechanical models, powered by a mainspring that had to be wound periodically by the wearer.

However, the rest of the watch manufacturing industry embraced the new technology. Particularly in the Far East, companies discovered that quartz watches could be produced much cheaper, display a trendier look, and still keep extremely accurate time. By 1992, Hong Kong alone was producing one fifth of the world's watches. The Japanese firms of Seiko, Citizen, and Casio also accounted for a major bulk of the world market in watches. Consumers had decided that they were not going to pay for Swiss quality when they could get the same for much cheaper prices elsewhere.

The Swiss watch firms were hard hit. By the end of the 1970s, their market share had dropped to 15 percent, and over one third of the watch companies went out of business. Facing extinction, the two largest Swiss companies, ASUAG and SSIH, merged in 1983 to form SMH, the Swiss Corporation for Microelectronics and Watchmaking Industries. They brought in a Lebanese-born management consultant to the Swiss watch industry as CEO of the new company—Nicholas Hayek.

Being an outsider, Hayek had the advantage of looking at the problem with fresh eyes. He realized that times had changed; people did not buy watches as functional time-telling devices but as fashion accessories. In the past, people often owned one watch for a lifetime, but because technology had drastically lowered the cost of watches, consumers enjoyed wearing a variety of timepieces. However, cheap watches looked cheap. Hayek came up with the idea for a Swatch brand—a very inexpensive but stylish watch with endless new designs that did much more than just tell time. It became a fashion phenomenon. (Though many think the word *Swatch* is a contraction meaning "Swiss Watch," Hayek claims it refers to "Second Watch," carrying with it the idea that a watch can be a casual, fun, and relatively disposable accessory.)

Swatch became a strong brand. Never before had cheap watches been marketed in such a way, but it worked. Because they were not expensive, consumers bought new ones to match their attire. It seemed so simple in retrospect; so why didn't the Chinese, Japanese, or Koreans develop a Swatch concept?

Probably because it would not have worked. Only the Swiss were strategically positioned to make such a move. Because Swatches were made in Switzerland, they enjoyed the residual goodwill of two centuries of national reputation in watch craftsmanship. But wasn't it a gamble to risk that reputation on a cheaper product?

Of course—which is why Nicholas Hayek was such a leader. He had the genius to recognize that the combination of style, variety, low price, and Swiss quality would be the key to pulling the Swiss watch industry out of its doldrums. They targeted sales of 1 million Swatch watches for 1983, the first year of sales, and 2.5 million in 1984.

But through aggressive marketing, particularly by trendy stores in the United States that sold only Swatch watches, the brand took off, even more than expected. In the first ten years, from 1983 to 1993, SMH sold more than 100 million Swatch watches.

Today, the Swatch Group remains the world's largest watch company, and though its sales have decreased in recent years, the Group has accelerated its acquisition of Swiss luxury brands and diversified its offerings considerably. Nicholas Hayek's leadership turned around a country's major industry!

Change That Did Not Work—The Union of Soviet Socialist Republics (USSR)

Winston Churchill once said that the Soviet Union was a riddle wrapped in a mystery inside an enigma. He could well have been speaking about the last premier of that nation, Mikhail Sergei Gorbachev. He appeared to be a product of the regime, joining the Communist Party at 21, completing his law degree at Moscow University at 22, serving in government positions and moving up through the party hierarchy, and eventually at age 49 becoming the youngest member of the Politburo. By all accounts, he should have followed the party line when he was handed the party chairmanship in 1985. Instead, he flew headlong against 70 years of Soviet tradition and embarked on a comprehensive program of political, economic, and social liberalization under the slogans of *glasnost* ("openness") and *perestroika* ("restructuring"). Yet these failed to produce the reforms that Gorbachev desired. Ironically, the one thing that he was able to accomplish was the process for his own demise from leadership and the dismantling of the country he led.

Mikhail Gorbachev had the fortune of being exactly at the right place at the right time. Leonid Brezhnev had served as the head of government from 1964 to 1982, and upon his death, Yuri Andropov was appointed as General Secretary. This was providential for Gorbachev, because Andropov was his mentor and was instrumental in his appointment to the Central Committee and later to the Politburo itself. But just two years later, in February 1984, Andropov died and Konstantin Chernenko was named to take his place. When Chernenko died just 13 months later in March 1985, the Central Committee realized that they needed to put into place a younger man for the sake of stability and continuity.

Mikhail Gorbachev seemed like a safe choice. He had served well within the Party, and had built up a reputation against corruption and inefficiency, both areas that needed constant attention in the Soviet system. But he had other qualities that spoke well of his leadership. He

93

had made some foreign trips, thanks to his mentor Andropov, and had appeared to carry himself well on the international stage. In a famous conversation between Margaret Thatcher and Gorbachev in December 1984 at Mrs. Thatcher's country residence Chequers, she commented, "He is a man we can do business with."

No one, including those living within the USSR, was prepared for what Gorbachev had in mind. When he first announced his twin ideals of *glasnost* and *perestroika*, most wrote it off as typical Soviet posturing. But the nuclear disaster at Chernobyl in 1986 forced Gorbachev to make good on his claims. The government began to relax restrictions on dissent and religious worship. Political prisoners began to be released, increased emigration (especially among Jews) was permitted, corruption was publicly condemned, and there was even some critical reexamination of Soviet history.

Gorbachev hoped that these changes would renew and enliven the Soviet system. He was wise enough to realize that the USSR desperately needed change. There were pressures everywhere. The ill-advised war with Afghanistan had been very costly, not just in military resources but also in public opinion both at home and abroad.

President Reagan in the United States made no secret of his animosity, calling the USSR an "evil empire" and devoting enormous funds toward technology that could render the Soviet nuclear arsenal obsolete. The Soviet economy staggered along, but seemed hopelessly out-of-date when compared with the West.

Throughout his six years in office, Gorbachev pushed hard for changes, hoping to make significant reforms, so that the system would work more efficiently and more democratically. He wanted to change the political, military, and economic structure of his country all at once. Yet he could not control the process. He moved too fast for the party regulars who were concerned about their loss of privilege and status, but moved too slow for radical reformers who hoped to do away with the one-party state and the command economy altogether. He received recognition for making strides in reducing the arms race with the United States; but many military leaders in his own country saw this as a sellout, and many in the West saw it as expediency due to the emergence of American technical superiority.

Time had also run out on the Soviet experiment. After seven decades of promise of the "workers' paradise," the workers were getting a bit restless. With the free flow of information increasing in the 1980s, it was no longer possible to convince Soviet citizens that they lived in the best country in the world. Gorbachev tried to make market reforms, but again, these seemed to only tantalize rather than satisfy the increasingly impatient populace.

The change simply did not work—at least not as Gorbachev intended. In August 1991, while Gorbachev was on vacation in the Crimea, the hard-liners pulled a coup; and although it failed, it was obvious that the forces of change that Gorbachev had unleashed were now working against him. At the end of the year, Gorbachev was forced to resign as president of a Soviet Union no longer in existence. Change did not reform the system as Gorbachev intended; instead, it caused its collapse. Rather than being heralded as a great reformer, through most of the 1990s, many Russians blamed him for their political and economic turmoil.

Change in Progress—The United States Armed Forces

With the collapse of the Soviet Union, the United States faced a unique problem. It had developed a military machine that far exceeded any conceivable foe. In the Gulf War in 1991, the United States military completely overwhelmed the Iraqi Army on their own soil in exactly 100 hours of active fighting. The U.S. had unquestionably the best military might in the world.

But for some years before, there were visible cracks in this great fortress. For one thing, there had been frustration in Congress and among certain military officers dating back to the Vietnam War concerning what they believed to be the poor quality in military advice available to civilian decision-makers. There was also the problem of the linear alignment of the US forces. Because of their structure, it was necessary to "deconflict" when engaging an enemy, which meant that in the first Gulf War, the Marines were given a certain area of engagement, the Army another, and the coalition forces still another. The ammunition of one branch of service was incompatible with the weapons of another.

After several years of hearings, the Goldwater-Nichols Department of Defense Reorganization Act of 1986 was enacted. Even though it was passed five years before the Gulf War engagement, it was obvious that the multiservice operations aspect still had yet to be realized.

Though victorious, the US military was still using old operating concepts in sequential phases and massed formations. Military leaders realized that they needed more than just a new structural design; they needed to change an entire military culture.

That culture was famous for wanting to prepare to fight the last war, not the next one. An insightful editorial in a major defense magazine noted that there have been ten comparable military transformations in the past 700 years, such as the use of the longbow, which led to British victories at Crecy and Agincourt, and Nazi Germany's use of blitzkrieg concepts to defeat Poland, France, and the Benelux countries in 1939-1940. At the same time, history also shows that major mistakes have been made in dealing with military transformation.[2]

History took a turn on September 11, 2001. President Bush noted in his address at The Citadel on December 11, 2001, "The need for military transformation was clear before the conflict in Afghanistan, and before September 11th....What's different today is our sense of urgency—the need to build this future force while fighting a present war. It's like overhauling an engine while you're going at 80 miles an hour. Yet we have no other choice."[3]

The U.S. military faces several challenges. First, they must clearly identify who and what they are up against. As recently as March 2005, the chairman of the Joint Chiefs of Staff stated, "The transformation of the United States military (today) is to get ready for what's around the next corner, and this is difficult, because we don't know what is around the next corner."[4] The enemy keeps transforming as well.

The second challenge is to enact major transformation changes within the military structure, while at the same time, maintain a high degree of readiness and effectiveness within those forces. To use President Bush's analogy of overhauling the engine, it is an almost impossible task. The U.S. Joint Forces Command, located in Norfolk, Virginia, has been instrumental in this regard. As David Fautua, special assistant to the Commander of UFCOM, has shared with me personally, thousands of key action officers have been oriented away from the "stovepipe" arrangement of their branch of service (as a stand-alone entity), and empowered with a "functionally-oriented cross-matrix comprehensive support system." This adaptive, collaborative environment has opened the door to overcoming the biggest challenge—culture.

Military officers who have developed their careers in one system are not so quick to want to jump into another. There is an old adage that says if something is not broken, do not attempt to fix it. To many within the military in the United States, this position of strength has worked in America's favor and should be maintained. But the momentum of transformation has been in full force for nearly a decade now, and though no one knows what the end product will exactly look like, it should be a definite improvement on what it looks like today.

So How to Change?

As President Bush noted in the quote above, the wise leader understands that he or she has no choice. In this day and age of rapid change taking place in all aspects of society and life, to fail to embrace change is to sign a death warrant for a company or organization.

Edmund Burke, the famous British politician commented that healthy "change is the means of our preservation." William Safire, columnist for the *New York Times* said it best, "When you are through changing, you are through."

As a final thought, a leader who is leading people who have been provoked into discomfort will usually find him or herself quite unpopular. Jack Welch was vilified during the 1980s and early 1990s for "wrecking" a beautiful company like GE. He took the heat and GE profited greatly as a result.

No less an authority than Niccolo Machiavelli has noted, "There is no more delicate matter to take in hand, nor many dangerous to conduct, nor more doubtful of success, than *to step up as a leader in the introduction of change*. For he who innovates will have for his enemies all those who are well off under the existing order of things, and only lukewarm support in those who might be better off under the new."[5]

Neil Postman, media theorist, cultural critic, and professor at New York University, noted that no great religious leader, from Buddha to Moses to Jesus to Mohammed to Luther, ever offered people what they wanted—only what they needed.

Real leaders see the light—and then feel the heat!

Endnotes

1. Clark, Liz. *The Essence of Change* (Prentice Hall, Englewood Cliffs, NJ, 1994).

2. "Observations on Military Transformation" *Defense Watch*. Vol. 216, (December 23, 2002).

3. Quoted in "Military Transformation: A Strategic Approach" publication of the Office of Force Transformation (May 2003).

4. Myers, Richard B., Air Force General, press release of Armed Forces press service (March 21, 2005).

5. Machiavelli, Niccolo, translated by Adams, Robert M., *The Prince* (W. W. Norton, New York, NY , 1977).

Key Ideas

1. Followers are *comfortable*: result of status quo, contentment with present conditions, security in the knowledge of the known and expected, relaxed about the future, unnecessary to plan—resulting in resistance to change.

2. Followers are *uncomfortable*: result of dissatisfaction with the status quo due to either perceived beneficial gain or detrimental threat in the future, concerns about the unexpected, anxiety about the future, necessary to make decisions involving risk and loss—resulting in an openness and desire to change, with the purpose to bring back state of "comfort."

3. Initiating change in an organization requires a leader to build a strong support group for the change, due to the fact that there will always be a contingent who will not support the change, and could actually tip the balance away from the proposed direction and toward maintaining the status quo.

Questions for Active Leaders

1. Given a particular change situation you have faced, how could "promise of gain" have been used rather than "threat of loss"?

2. Considering Liz Clark's Change Formula, what is required to access the practicality of the change (minimum risk/disruption)?

Questions for FLOWters (Future Leaders of the World)

1. When was the last time you changed something in your life? What was it? What were the factors? How do you think this could relate to developing your leadership skills?

2. Think of a time when you were able to persuade a friend towards a particular course of action? What were the influencing factors? Do these relate to leadership?

CHAPTER FIVE

The Third Essential—
The Factors of Condition

The Circumstances of Leadership

Leadership has been described as something like the abominable snowman. There are footprints to prove that he has been around, but no one has actually seen him. Elements of Leadership Capital are the footprints that indicate evidence of leadership. When we see the competencies such as wisdom and voice in action, we admire them and even often take them for granted. It is only over a period of time, and perhaps even after the individual has departed, that we begin to recognize that we were in the presence of a leader.

Michael Jordan is generally considered one of the greatest basketball players ever to have played the game. Yet it took him some time before his greatness was realized. He actually failed to make his high school basketball team as a youth, but later developed well enough to be considered for a scholarship to a major college. He went to the University of North Carolina to play basketball after his first two choices, UCLA and Virginia, turned him down. When he left the University of North Carolina in 1984 to enter the National Basketball Association, he was selected by the Chicago Bulls as the third person in the NBA draft of college players. Though one sports magazine had named him Player of the Year for two years running, and he had been cocaptain of the U.S.A.'s gold medal Olympic team at Los Angeles, most experts considered Jordan an extremely talented player but not the best pro prospect coming out of college that year. No one foresaw that this individual would later become a living legend, the epitome of basketball excellence.

Jordan's early career was successful from an individual standpoint. In 1986, he scored an NBA playoff-record 63 points in one game against Boston, but his team still lost. In 1987, he won his first NBA scoring title and was the first guard in league history to record 200 steals and 100 blocks in one season. In 1988, he was named the league's most valuable player. But despite all these individual heroics, Jordan's team, the Chicago Bulls, never advanced to the final round of the playoff championships. His greatness was still not recognized; it seemed as though he would follow other NBA stars who had also led the league for a number of years and were later forgotten.

It was not until 1991, when the management of his team finally assembled a formidable alliance of players around Jordan that he took on an almost supernatural status. His team won the NBA championship three years in a row, from 1991–1994, an unprecedented accomplishment since the 1960s. Then after two years of "retirement" to play baseball, he came back and accomplished the same feat again—three consecutive NBA championships!

Michael Jordan perfectly represents the principle that Conditions control Capital. The reason no one recognized the superstar potential within Jordan while he played in college was because Coach Dean Smith ran a very tightly controlled offense centered on team play that discouraged individuals from standing out. Coach Smith emphasized teamwork, which meant that a thoroughbred like Jordan had to get hitched up to the wagon just like the other horses. Once in the NBA, however, individual achievement was encouraged and he began to show his real talent. But again, until he had a supporting team around him, he could not achieve ultimate success. In fact, he actually had to do less to achieve more. Jordan averaged 32 points per game before his team won a championship in the 1980s, yet during the championship run of the 1990s, he averaged 30 points per game.

Exactly the same thing is true in leadership. Individuals may have latent within them extraordinary talents and abilities (Leadership Capital), but until the Conditions are right, they will languish on the periphery of success. Unlike Leadership Capital, which can be developed, Leadership Conditions are largely outside the control of the individual. They are primarily sociological conditions that serve as catalysts to propel a leader into the limelight.

Though it is popular motivational hype that we can control our circumstances, the truth is that circumstances almost always find us. In most countries in the world we can choose where we live, where we work, the spouse we want to marry, the clothes we wear, the food we eat, etc. But cut very close to those choices and we discover that our options are often severely limited. Though we can theoretically live where we want, we know that economic conditions and opportunity predetermine our residence a great deal. The same is true with work options and almost every other choice we make in our lives.

Simply put, these conditions work for us or against us. In terms of leadership, they work for individuals to propel them into a leadership relationship with their followers, or they work against them preventing it from happening. It is like the movie character Forrest Gump. He was a simpleton who had an ability to run fast, and ended up on a championship football team. He went to Vietnam and became a war hero doing what came naturally, running and saving his friends during a bombing. During his recovery from an injury, he learned ping-pong and became a celebrity when he was one of the first Americans to visit Red China. Later, he starts a shrimp business, which nearly goes bankrupt, until a storm beaches the other ships, and his boat is able to bring in the big hauls. By simply acting like himself, but being in the right place at the right time, he enjoyed remarkable success.

Conditions will propel anyone into authority. As Desmond Tutu commented, "I became a leader by default since nature does not allow a vacuum." If strong Leadership Capital is present, then individuals can use the opportunity presented by the conditions and take the organization forward in a positive direction. However, if Leadership Capital is deficient, then individuals will misuse the opportunity and seek to satisfy their own need for power, prestige, financial gain, or other benefits.

The conditions are the four proper P's: *place*, *position*, *period*, and *people*. Conditions are catalysts to action. In large part, they are beyond our control. Any individual who wants to aspire to leadership development must recognize these Conditions to know when and how they may be working for or against them.

Place: The Domain of Leadership

The condition of place refers to the particular area of expertise that the leader holds. Some leaders are very "domain specific," meaning they are very good within the narrow confines of their specialty, while others are able to "cross domains," meaning they can go from one field to another with equal effectiveness.

Michael Jordan was the preeminent basketball player of his day, possibly of all time, but it seems that after his first three championships, he became bored with the game. He wanted a new challenge, so he turned to baseball. The Chicago White Sox immediately signed him and probably salivated at the thought of the increased sales they would see when he was playing for the home team in Chicago.

But first, Jordan had to make the team, which meant he had to prove his worth on what are called the "farm clubs." These are the minor league teams, generally located in smaller cities throughout the US that develop players for the major leagues. Jordan played for two years, but never could make the home club. Though it seemed hard to believe, Michael Jordan was quite ordinary when he got off the basketball court. Within his domain, he was the greatest. He could not transfer those incredible athletic abilities that he used on the basketball court, however, to the baseball diamond.

A business example of the same phenomenon is John Sculley. Sculley had made a turnaround as CEO of PepsiCo, narrowing the gap between them and their main competitor, Coca-Cola. From there Sculley went on to become chairman of Apple, and his success there made him one of the most admired leaders in the corporate world. Then in early 1983, IBM was looking for a new leader, and Sculley's name came up.

Instead, Sculley went to become chairman and chief executive at Spectrum Information Technologies, an obscure Long Island, New York firm. One of the top names of corporate America was joining what one journal described as a "tiny wireless-technology company that had no profits, no profile, and a checkered past...." Strangely, after only four months, Sculley quit. It turned out that he was unable to work with the company president and had totally misjudged the viability of his new company. *Newsweek* magazine featured a headline "From Champ to Chump."

Sculley was in the wrong place with Spectrum, whereas Apple and PepsiCo worked well for him. Why? It was probably because the latter two companies were more established and more suited to his executive style, whereas the smaller and more entrepreneurial Spectrum was not.

Leaders need to know where they are at their best. The three primary considerations for the domain of leadership place are culture, career, and organizational size.

Culture and Place

Edgar Schein, a corporate culture expert, notes that there are three different types of culture, and it is not difficult to surmise that each of these cultures has its own type of leader.[1]

- The first is the *operator culture*, where operational success is the key. These would be companies such as Motorola and Siemens.

- The second type is the *engineering culture*, where designers and technocrats drive the core technologies of the organization. These would be companies such as Toshiba, Bayer, and 3M.

- The third type is the *executive culture*, which is formed by executive management, the CEO, and immediate subordinates. These would be companies such as GE, Mars, Microsoft, and to a lesser extent, Virgin Atlantic.

Leaders who work well in an operational culture, with emphasis on quality control and systems management, might find the transition to an engineering culture, which stresses innovation, more than a bit difficult.

What worked best for them before would not work best now. Leaders need to know in what culture they best fit.

Career and Place

This idea of cultural fit might also relate to another of Schein's concepts, which is the "career anchor."[2] He states that a mature person has an underlying career value that he will not surrender. These include:

- *Technical / Functional* anchor—the quest to be an expert, the fulfillment that comes from the work itself.

- *General Managerial* anchor—the drive to climb the corporate ladder, more of a generalist than a technical / functional individual.

- *Autonomy / Independence* anchor—the desire to be free of organizational rules and restrictions, to be free to innovate and create.

- *Entrepreneurial Creativity* anchor—the strong desire to own and operate an enterprise or organization.

- *Security / Stability* anchor—the need to succeed for the purpose of relaxing, enjoying life, and not being pressured by financial burdens.

- *Service / Dedication* to a Cause anchor—the longing to make the world a better place, to help others, to solve societies' problems, etc.

- *Pure Challenge* anchor—the passion to do the difficult, to win out over the impossible.

- *Lifestyle* anchor—the desire to balance and integrate personal needs, family needs, and career goals.

Schein's career anchor theory may also explain why some individuals just do not seem to "fit" in certain places, even when they seem to have the right credentials for the job. Sir Isaac Newton, for example, was obviously a man driven to do the impossible. He solved seemingly insurmountable problems in physics and science. But the challenges of legislation are very different. They require more of a technician, particularly in the field of law. As a member of the British Parliament, Newton could not utilize his gifts, and as a result, was totally ineffective.

Size and Place

Another consideration is the size of the organization. I have noticed this about my own public speaking. For many years, I have been teaching and lecturing to gatherings as small as two and three people and groups as large as several thousand people. I have discovered that I have an "optimum" size that is about 15 to 20 individuals. With that size group, I can personally interact with each individual and assess if I am reaching him or her with my information.

The reason for this particular ideal size group is because I know that, in my heart, I am a teacher. I love to teach. So the right place for me is to teach in a setting with a small, classroom-size group. Now, this is not to mean that I cannot teach larger groups. In fact, I am often called to teach or lecture to large auditoriums of people. I may even do it well (so I am told). But the size of the group does affect how I teach, and even what I teach.

Leaders face the same conditions. Everyone has an optimum size organization where they feel comfortable. When they are in this domain, they seem to flourish. But organizations are not stagnant, and especially if the leader is successful, the organization will grow in size. If this happens rapidly, it often presents a problem of adjustment for the leader. Some are able to adjust, and some do not.

This relates back to the infamous Peter Principle, developed by Laurence J. Peter (1919-1990), a Canadian academic. Peter noted that individuals will be promoted as a result of their competence, but when they can no longer perform adequately, they will stop being promoted. He thus postulated the Peter Principle that managers in an organization rise up to their level of incompetence. "If at first you don't succeed, you may be at your level of incompetence."

If leaders are in their optimum domain, they can flourish. In one sense, people are like wine. Each variety of grape has a certain climate and soil where it can best grow. As was so beautifully described in the 2004 film, *Sideways*, some varieties, like the Cabernet Sauvignon, are rather versatile and grow in many different places. Others, like the Pinot Noir, are rather temperamental and can grow only in very select environments. People are the same way. Everyone has a "best" place where he or she can thrive—although some are more versatile than others.

It takes a high degree of self-awareness on the part of leaders to determine exactly where this "place" is for them. What organizational culture matches their personality, what career path should they take given their particular career anchor, and what size company or organization do they best fit? If a person is serious about leading, he should make every effort to get in a place where he can do so.

Position: The Authority of the Leader

An individual's position is also critical. It might seem too obvious to state, but without ever being given the opportunity to lead others, it is impossible to do so. Surveys show that the reason many individuals seek to be entrepreneurs is not as much for reasons of wealth as they want to be their own bosses. They are convinced that they are never given the proper forum they need to lead others. Mary Kay Ash found her path to promotion blocked because she was a woman, so at the age of 45, she founded her own company, May Kay Cosmetics, which has become one of the major cosmetic companies in the world.

Position refers to the authority that the leader possesses. Very simply, the greater the authority vested in the leader, the greater his or her influence to make changes within the organization. A typical question I always ask when I first speak with a manager of a department or a division chief is to find out precisely what they are able to change within their area of responsibility. Do they have discretion over salaries or the giving of bonuses? Can they change an operation or procedure without approval from a higher authority? Can they restructure or realign personnel freely? All of these questions are designed to identify their degree of strength in the conditional area of leadership position.

Leadership, as opposed to anti-leadership, utilizes authority to draw followers voluntarily rather than compelling them. This is done through the two types of power or authority that a leader possesses: position power and personal power.

The power referred to above is position power, which is vested through the organizational structure. It comes from the top down. Personal power, on the other hand, is given from the bottom up. This is the respect that followers have for another individual. These two types of power go hand in hand, for if individuals have the position but not the respect of those they are in authority over, they must use control measures to insure that their will is done. On the other hand, if individuals have personal power only, they may not have the proper influence to accomplish what needs to be done.

Lee Iacocca: Study in Position

An interesting character study in how an increase in position is directly proportional to the impact of a leader is Lee Iacocca. His story is well-known given his rather public persona and that his book, *Iacocca: An Autobiography* (Bantam, 1986), is one of the best-selling business biographies of all time.

As a manager, Iacocca used as much discretion as he was allowed to get results. In 1956, his district was last in car sales. He decided to introduce a new program called "56 for 56." He made it possible to purchase a new 1956 Ford for 20 percent down and monthly payments of $56 for three years. The program was a huge success, catapulting his district from last place in sales to first.

He was promoted to management at Ford's home office in Detroit and was given the task of heading up the Fairlane Committee. This committee used market and demographic research data to decide what type of new car to produce. Their demographic research revealed that there would be a sharp increase in the number of young adults between 18 and 34, and economic indicators pointed toward increased family incomes through the 1960s. They considered the sociological impact of these factors and concluded that women probably would be buying more cars and that more families would have two cars.

The Fairlane Committee then strategized what type of car would have the most appeal given these new factors. The car had to be small, but also needed to comfortably seat four passengers. It had to be light, inexpensive, and yet appeal to several markets (meaning it could just as easily go to the church or country club as the drag strip). But Iacocca's experience with car buyers also told him that with this one basic design, there needed to be a wide range of options so that the customer could buy as much luxury as he or she could afford.

The end product was the 1964 Mustang. It was a revolutionary design and quite a gamble for Ford, but Iacocca was able to sell top management on the idea. They were not unhappy that he did, because the Mustang model was a huge success. Iacocca was handed the presidency just six years later based on the success of this car.

As president of Ford, Iacocca had more positional power, but it was still limited. He was able to initiate a program called "Shuck the Losers." This program gave managers three years to make their departments profitable or sell them off. Yet when he proposed partnering with Honda to produce cars and develop a minivan, he was shot down by the chairman of the board, Henry Ford II.

Iacocca's difficulties with Henry Ford II continued to escalate until he was finally fired in July 1978. Just four months later, he took on the CEO position of the Chrysler Corporation. Chrysler was on the verge of bankruptcy, and it seemed there was little that would save it. Iacocca took the revolutionary step of appealing to the government for backed loans to get out of the financial crisis. He did hard bargaining with one of the toughest unions in America for cuts in salary and benefits. But he also showed he was personally committed by reducing his salary to exactly $1.00 per year.

It all worked. Chrysler began putting out cars that were competitive and profitable for the company. The company was able to pay back all its government loans by July 1983. Iacocca was recognized as one of the miracle workers of the corporate world.

But it was not until he had the full positional power at Chrysler that he was truly able to demonstrate his full leadership capital. At the same time, he would not have risen to the heights of positional power had his personal power not been as strong as it was. Personal power brings respect and influence on a personal basis. Positional power brings the authority to implement change and impact the direction of the organization.

Leaders must possess authority—that is what differentiates them from followers. Persons may languish for years without ever getting the opportunity to lead because they never are in a position to do so.

As we have noted several times, this opportunity is largely circumstantial. It will come when it comes. The important thing is to be ready when it does.

Period: The Times of the Leader

The times in which the leader lives: the economic, social, and political situations will greatly influence the impact and influence that individuals can have on their organizations. The accounting profession is one example of how a period has effected and determined the destiny of those participating in it.

The 1494 publication in Venice of Luca Pacioli's *Summa di Arithmetica* was the first published work dealing with double-entry bookkeeping. For hundreds of years, the methodology of accounting was understood and practiced, but accounting professions did not materialize until the mid-19th century. The industrial revolution led to the development of joint stock companies and the growth of stock exchanges.

Suddenly, there was a need for standardized financial reporting. In 1845 William Deloitte opened an accounting office in London. In 1850 Samuel Price founded an accounting firm in London, and in 1865 he took on Edwin Waterhouse as a partner. William Cooper, the oldest son of a Quaker banker, formed his accountancy company in 1854.

The growth of railroads in the United States, largely built through British engineering, also facilitated the growth of accounting. Arthur Young, a Scotsman, opened his firm in Kansas City in 1895. The brothers, Alwin and Theodore Ernst of Cleveland, began their firm in 1903. William Lybrand, Edward Ross, and Robert Montgomery formed a company in 1898 that literally wrote the book on auditing. William Peat, a London accountant, joined up with Scottish-born James Marwick and Roger Mitchell in 1911, and their firm eventually evolved into KPMG International.

Could any of these men have begun the companies that bear their names had they not been born at a time when the accounting field was coming into its own? Were there no men in the 16th, 17th, or 18th centuries who matched their expertise and leadership in accounting? Or was it simply that such individuals were not fortunate enough to be living in the times where these skills and attributes would be acknowledged and needed?

To continue with the accounting firms example, the first half of the twentieth century saw very little change with the accounting world. Ernst & Young was known as "old reliable." Deloitte was known as the "Cadillac, not the Ford" of accounting. Arthur Anderson was seen as the innovator, entering the consulting business in 1954. Price Waterhouse was the formal and traditional giant, with 100 of the *Fortune 500* companies as clients in 1970. Few industries were considered as stable as the accounting field, known as the Big Eight. The CEOs of these firms knew their respective places and saw that there was little they could do to alter their position in the market.

But again, unique economic conditions were destined to play a hand. Savings and loan companies in the United States ran up atrocious debt that they were unable to recover. The U.S. Congress, financial investors, and government regulators were looking for someone to blame. For the first time, accounting firms were expected be held accountable for the veracity as well as the form of audited financial statements.

Legal action against the firms soared. Ernst & Young was forced to pay $400 million for allegedly mishandling the audits of four failed savings and loans. Deloitte was sued because of its actions relating to junk-bond king Michael Milken and the failure of several savings and loans. Arthur Anderson, Coopers and Lybrand, and Price Waterhouse all had to deal with expensive litigation in the 1980s and 1990s. The companies were forced into mergers for their own survival.

The times dictate the opportunities for the leader. Even within a field as seemingly stable as accounting, the period of time has great determination upon the impact of the leader. The leadership competencies needed to guide an accounting firm in 1900 were very different than in 1950 and still different in the year 2000. It is not enough to be the right man in the right place—it is also necessary to be there at the right time.

Sometimes individuals are simply ahead of their time. I personally know what it is like to be ahead of the market. I started an industrial safety and health consulting company with two other individuals in 1982 called COSMAT (Consultants in Occupational Safety Management and

Training). Industrial safety seemed very hot at the time because of a recent horrifying accident in Bhopal, India, involving the Union Carbide Company that killed hundreds. COSMAT provided assistance in complying with U.S. government requirements in safety and health for various industries, particularly in computer manufacturing, an area that generally thought of itself as a "clean" industry.

My role was in public relations, and my first job was to promote a need for our service by creating public awareness of employee health risks for those who worked with toxic substances. I wrote a number of different highly technical articles that were printed in industrial trade journals, and I was invited to speak at chamber of commerce meetings and other business forums. I was able to show how the costs of compliance were miniscule in comparison to the hazards of rising employee health benefits and the threat of government intervention.

In two years, I had become something of a recognized "expert" in the field of employee health related to toxic substances, even being called upon to confer with state and national government officials.

But despite major marketing efforts on our part and my relatively high profile, COSMAT went under after little more than two years. The target market just did not perceive its need for compliance to government regulations as a priority area of concern. Not too longer thereafter, however, the U.S. federal government began to strictly enforce Occupational Safety and Health Administration regulations by prosecuting some highly respected companies. That got management's attention. Five years after we closed our doors, several similar firms were making enormous profits doing exactly what we had proposed. The market had obviously changed its mind.

Understanding the times is critical for leaders, because they might be too early, and they might wait too long. Many times there might be only one right moment and it will not wait. Shakespeare wrote in *Julius Caesar*,

> *There is a tide in the affairs of men, which,*
> *taken at the flood, leads on to fortune*
> *omitted, all the voyage of their life is*
> *bound in shallows and in miseries.*
> *On such a full sea are we now afloat;*

and we must take the current when it serves,
or lose our ventures.

When there is a tide, do not be caught simply watching it.

People: The Followers of the Leader

Just as individuals do not usually get to pick the members of their family, so leaders many times do not get to handpick those who will follow them. Usually only in a start-up situation where entrepreneurs get to select the initial workers or on a special project do leaders have the luxury of choosing exactly those with whom they want to work. In most other situations, leaders must make the most of those whom they already have.

As the first two chapters reiterated, followers who do not want to be led will prevent the leader from being effective. In fact, they have the capacity to completely paralyze any efforts of the leader. The literature in this area of "followership" has developed in recent years almost as much as the subject of leadership itself.

For example, in the very fine compilation of leadership articles entitled *Contemporary Views in Leadership*, the second part immediately following the section on "Understanding Leadership" is called, "Followership: Making Leadership Possible."[3]

The emphasis on followers is a rather recent phenomenon in leadership, and the "father" of the followership movement is Robert Kelley, business professor at Carnegie-Mellon University in Pittsburgh, Pennsylvania. In his opinion, focusing on leaders is only one or two percent of the equation of leadership, and it is really followers who make up the 98 or 99 percent. They should be the focus.

Robert Kelley defines two dimensions of followers: 1. independence and critical thinking versus conformity of thought, and 2. activity versus passivity. These combine to make essentially five types of followers:

- Sheep: low in action and low in critical thinking.
- Yes People: active but uncritical.
- Alienated Followers: critical but do not act.
- Survivors: middle ground on both scales.

- Effective Followers: think for themselves and carry out tasks with commitment and enthusiasm.

The following chart illustrates this concept. If Kelley is correct in his assessment, the Sheep and Yes People are still followers of the leaders, albeit not effective ones. The Survivors can be influenced, which only leaves the Alienated Followers as the true problem.

	Critical	THOUGHT	Conformity
Activity			
	Effective Followers		Yes People
ACTIONS		Survivors	
	Alienated Followers		Sheep
Passivity			

Kelley's model is useful in that it helps explain the leadership condition of people. Though the present popular paradigm of leadership is that leaders are able to "transform" their followers, the reality is that leaders must have the right ingredients to work with in the first place. As I enjoy telling my students, you cannot put in what God left out. In some cases, there is something "left out" of followers that literally ties the hands of those who wish to lead them.

There is nothing new in this idea; in fact, it dates back as early as the ancient Greeks. In Plato's *Republic*, the first few paragraphs form a "framing scene" in which the seed of every idea that will be presented in the book is to be found. Socrates and his friend Glaucon are returning to their home after having visited the city of Ariston. They are stopped on the road by Polemarchus and a number of others.

They inform Socrates that he is wanted at the house of Cephalus, the father of Polemarchus. Socrates is not interested in going, and Polemarchus tells him, "Look around. There are more of us than there are of you."

Socrates is not interested in a confrontation, of course, and suggests that perhaps he would be able to persuade this group to let Glaucon and him go on their way. Polemarchus, obviously the spokesman for the group, asks how he will be able to persuade them if they do not want to listen. Glaucon admits that there is no way. In other words, if no one will listen to Socrates, no one will follow.

This classic scene is a microcosm of the dialectic between force and persuasion. If the followers do not want to follow, they are not going to follow. Only the use of force can move people against their will.

The Barriers of Persuasion

What prevents individuals from being persuaded or led by another? There are many possible causes, but they all essentially boil down into factual, emotional, and ethical reasons as perceived by the followers.

Factual reasons relate to logic. This means that it is difficult to follow an individual who is perceived as not up to the task of leading. Older people often resist younger leaders for this reason. They do not respect the intellectual expertise or experience base of the prospective leader enough to put their trust in them. In one of my leadership classes, the question came up of a 22 year old responsible for supervising workers in their 50s. I doubted that this obstacle could ever be completely overcome, for the simple reason that the older workers are never going to be able to "look up" to someone so much younger than them.

Emotional reasons cover a host of problems: cultural differences, gender differences, even political differences. One large international hotel opened in Riga and found that while their international trainers had little difficulty with the lower-skilled nationals, they had enormous tension with the higher-skilled professional nationals. The lower-skilled workers did not question the experts from abroad, and took everything they were told as gospel. The professionals, on the other hand, felt demeaned by their trainers and resented it very much.

This is one reason that cross-cultural training has become so important in recent years. As professionals from different countries are interacting more than ever before, it is essential that they know how to be culturally sensitive. I once listened to one professor from the United States give a lecture that was laced with illustrations of baseball and popular American television programs. His audience was very astute and intellectual. They could understand the words, but not the context. In one sense, this is an example of cultural blindness, as the professor assumed the audience should know about the references he was making.

Ethical reasons also can cover a wide range of conditions. If followers perceive that their boss has widely divergent ethical parameters from them, they are not going to trust that individual as a leader. Again, this can be for cross-cultural reasons. What is considered highly unethical in the United States, like paying off an official for better considerations, is generally accepted in other parts of the world.

However, given all that has been said, the leadership condition of people is probably the one condition that can be influenced more than the other three.

Even the hardest of souls can warm up after a period of time. Leaders should not simply wash their hands and declare that "these people are hopeless." Maybe the fault is that the leader does not understand them well enough. As Abraham Lincoln once said, "I don't like that man; I need to get to know him better."

The Right Man at the Right Time

How does a person achieve greatness? Is it enough to be rich, wise, and ambitious? No, for if the conditions are not right, nothing substantial can be forthcoming. History is filled with such examples, but Alexander Fleming, the discoverer of penicillin, is perhaps the best illustration. Here was a man, the seventh of eight children, born on a small farm in a remote, rural part of Scotland, who lost his father at a young age, yet became one of the greatest men of the 20th century. His story demonstrates the importance of leadership conditions.

Alexander Fleming (1881–1955) was 14 years old when his father died, and he decided to move to London where his brother Tom had opened a medical practice. After attending a polytechnic school, Alex (as he was known) was encouraged by his brother to enter business, which he did for four years. Working at a shipping firm turned out to be uninteresting for him, so in 1900, when the Boer War broke out between Great Britain and its colonies in southern Africa, Alex and two of his brothers joined a Scottish regiment.

It was more of a sporting club, however, because they never went to Africa, but they did get in a great deal of shooting, swimming, and even water polo. Water polo would turn out to have a providential effect in Alexander Fleming's life. When his uncle died and left each of the children 250 pounds sterling, Alex decided to take up medicine. He had top scores in the qualifying exams, and even though he had his choice of schools, he selected St. Mary's because it was the only school he was familiar with, having had played against them in water polo.

The hunting experience also played a role in his medical career. In 1905, Fleming planned to specialize in surgery, and when his initial training was complete, he would leave St. Mary's. However, the captain of the St. Mary's Rifle Club was anxious to keep Alex on the team because he was such a great shot, so he convinced Alex to leave surgery and go into immunology, the department that, coincidentally, was headed by this same rifle club captain. It apparently suited Fleming, for he would stay there for the rest of his career.

Fleming distinguished himself as a capable researcher, but it was not until 1928 that he made the discovery for which he is most noted. He was straightening up some examination dishes, where he had been growing staphylococcus bacteria, which were piled in a sink. The bacteria had grown some mold around them (obviously he was not the most careful of housekeepers), but what got his attention was that in the region of the culture just surrounding the mold, the bacteria had been dissolved. He took a sample of the mold and found that it was from the penicillium family, later specified as penicillium notatum.

From there began a long and laborious process that eventually resulted in the drug known as penicillin. It has become one of the most important and widely used antibiotics in the world, saving literally millions of lives. Fleming was awarded the Nobel Prize for his discovery in 1945.

Alexander Fleming's life is a marvel of circumstances and good fortune. His father died, yet it enabled him to leave rural Scotland and move to London. He was bored with business and went into the army, but stayed out of the war and developed his sports skills.

This sporting background led him to the institution that he worked with his entire life. The happenstance of the dirty dishes led to one of the most important medical discoveries of the century. As Fleming himself said, "One sometimes finds what one is not looking for."

Leadership Conditions are the serendipity of life. They are not unlike the playing field for an athletic contest. The players each have their own skills and abilities, their athletic capital, but they must use these skills on the field of play. That field may not be in the best of condition, but, for better or worse, that is where the game is played. The field conditions may very well favor one team more than the other. (This is popularly known as "home field advantage.")

Leaders must know what those field conditions are, recognize how to take advantage of them, and when to not fight against what they cannot change. Leaders who have developed their Leadership Capital will be ready to take hold of the reigns of power when the conditions are right.

In the film *Last Samurai*, the warlord Katsumoto asks Captain Algren, "You believe a man can change his destiny?" Algren answers, "No. I think a man can only do what he can, until his destiny is revealed."

Circumstances do not make a man—they reveal him.

Endnotes

1. Schein, *Edgar. Organizational Culture and Leadership.* (Jossey-Bass, San Francisco, 1985).

2. Schein, Edgar. *Career Anchors: Discovering Your Real Values*, revised edition. (Jossey-Bass, San Francisco, 1990).

3. Rosenbach, William E. and Taylor, Robert L., ed. *Contemporary Views in Leadership*, 3rd Edition, (Westview, Boulder, CO, 2001).

Key Ideas

1. Conditions are the sociological factors that serve as a catalyst to determine whether leadership can be exerted within an organization or group. These are people (the followers of the leader), place (the domain that "fits" the leader), period (the opportune time for the leader's initiative), and position (the amount of authority possessed by the leader.)

2. Place—impacted by the compatibility to corporate culture, the career anchor of the leader, and the size of the organization.

3. Position—impacted by the personal and positional power of the leader.

4. Period—impacted by hitting the right "tide," which is neither too soon or too late to initiate a change.

5. People—impacted by the degree of "followership" and the followers' willingness to be persuaded due to factual, emotional, and ethical reasons.

Questions for Active Leaders

1. Of the four leadership conditional areas, which do you believe offers the greatest hindrance to your leadership? What could you do, if anything, to increase your condition to lead?

2. Many management experts emphasize the need to spend time with followers as an important means to supervision and motivation. How could increased awareness help overcome factual, emotional, and ethical barriers?

Questions for FLOWters (Future Leaders of the World)

1. What do you believe would be the best "place" for you to lead? Try to describe your ideal working environment or situation.

2. Pick out a leader you know and analyze his or her Leadership Conditions.

CHAPTER SIX

The Fourth Essential—
The Foundations of Capital

Leader in Action

Already a celebrated polar explorer, Sir Ernest Shackleton coordinated the British Imperial Trans-Antarctic Expedition with the goal of accomplishing the first crossing of the Antarctic continent, a feat he considered to be the last great polar journey of the "Heroic Age of Exploration."

In December 1914, Shackleton set sail with his 27-man crew, many of whom, it is said, had responded to the following recruitment notice: "Men wanted for hazardous journey. Small wages. Bitter cold. Long months of complete darkness. Constant danger. Safe return doubtful. Honour and recognition in case of success. —Ernest Shackleton."

Ice conditions were unusually harsh, and the wooden ship (which Shackleton had renamed *Endurance* after his family motto, *Fortitudine Vincimus*—"By endurance we conquer") became trapped in the pack ice of the Weddell Sea. For ten months, the *Endurance* drifted, locked within the ice, until the pressure crushed the ship. With meager food, clothing, and shelter, Shackleton and his men were stranded on the ice floes, where they camped for five months.

When they had drifted to the northern edge of the pack, encountering open leads of water, the men sailed the three small lifeboats they had salvaged to a bleak crag called Elephant Island. They were on land for the first time in 497 days; however, it was uninhabited, and due to its distance from shipping lanes, provided no hope for rescue.

Recognizing the severity of the physical and mental strains on his men, Shackleton and five others immediately set out to take the crew's rescue into their own hands. In a 22-foot lifeboat named the *James Caird*, they accomplished the impossible, surviving a 17-day, 800-mile journey through the world's worst seas to South Georgia Island, where a whaling station was located.

The six men landed on an uninhabited part of the island, however, so their last hope was to cross 26 miles of mountains and glaciers, considered impassable, to reach the whaling station on the other side. Starved, frostbitten, and wearing rags, Shackleton and two others made the trek across the island, and in August 1916, 21 months after the initial departure of the *Endurance*, Shackleton himself returned to rescue the men on Elephant Island. Although they had withstood the most incredible hardship and privation, not one member of the 28-man crew was lost.

Many years after the events of the *Endurance*, the men were asked what kept them going during those long, dark months of despair. Their unanimous response was a single word, "Shackleton."

Some Make It and Some Don't

The Shackleton story has become something of a legend in business training evidenced by the proliferation of books, videos, and case studies that have been written on the Endurance Expedition in just the past decade.[1] Perhaps the reason is that this man so clearly made a difference. Never once in all his Antarctic expeditions did he ever lose a life. Under some of the most severe conditions on the planet, he was able to accomplish great goals, yet not compromise his core value—the safety of his men as the first priority. He did this by learning from mistakes, his own and others, practicing unwavering courage, and building trust by his every action around his men. In leading his Antarctic expeditions, Ernest Shackleton epitomized Ideal Leadership.

Leadership is not to be understood as some abstract formula, but in the living dimension of real people. The Interdisciplinary or Ideal Leadership Model examines individuals and determines their leadership *purpose, presence,* and *principles,* which make up their present capabilities and capacity for growth. These are termed their Leadership Capital. This Capital is not simply natural-born instincts. A person's life experiences and knowledge accumulate into a deposit, which will later serve him or her in a leadership role when the conditions become right. By calling it Leadership Capital, we are stating that it is a measurable component and that it can be developed.

For decades, leadership models have struggled with exactly how to factor in the serendipity element to leadership. It is not always the smartest, or boldest, or shrewdest individual who becomes the best leader. It is often a combination of these elements that serve them. Also, due to the undiscerning conditions of leadership—the smartest, boldest, or shrewdest may never have the opportunity to become a leader.

The most vivid example I witnessed of this phenomenon was in my earlier years when I had the opportunity of working with an elderly gentleman named Frank. He was unquestionably the smartest person I have ever known in my life. Select any subject from classical music to quantum mechanics and Frank could debate with the best of them. Frank never pursued advanced degrees because he felt he had nothing to learn at the university. One professor decided to take up Frank's challenge and arranged for him to take graduate exams in chemistry, physics, world literature, political science, and biology. Every night for weeks he went to the university and took these exams. When the results came in, Frank was in the top ten percentile in every subject.

He read more than anyone I ever met. He seemed to be capable of reading five or six books a day! His knowledge of medicine was so extensive that he once had a vehement argument with his doctor over some medication that the specialist was prescribing for him. Frank cited recent medical research, and when the doctor looked it up, he found Frank was right.

Frank was a genius. He held over 40 patents. He pioneered work in several different fields of electronics. His mental prowess was unquestioned. Besides that, Frank was also a very personable man. He was a friendly, warm, and engaging conversationalist. Almost everyone respected Frank. He had all the personal characteristics one would expect to find in an outstanding leader.

Yet, after a lifetime of hard work, with all his incredible knowledge and skills, he had almost nothing to show for it all. Circumstances worked against the man time and again. Through virtually no fault of his own (illnesses, changing market conditions, changes in government relations, unsavory working partners), the conditions played havoc with his life. In another place and another time, Frank might have become acknowledged as one of the great men of the 20th century. Instead, he was a nice, smart old man who never seemed to get a break. It is not fair—but that is life. It happens.

Conditions determine who gets the opportunity to lead. If conditions had placed Frank in a time when his gifts would have made an impact, among people who could work well with him, in a position of influence, he might have become recognized as one of the leading industrial scientists of his age. The fact that this did not happen is a caution to all of us that having Leadership Capital will never be good enough by itself.

But cases like Frank are rare. Some people do seem like they were born under an unlucky star, and that is unfortunate. What is true for most people, though, is that usually, sometime in life, they will get their shot at the top. The Book of Proverbs states, *"A man's gift makes room for him and brings him before great men"* (Prov. 18:16 NKJV). Generally speaking, quality of competence is appreciated by others and often leads to opportunity.

The right attitude is to focus on what can be changed, not on what cannot. Leadership Capital remains within the domain of the individual, and this is what we need to focus on in the fourth essential of leadership, the foundation of Capital.

Leadership Capital

Human anatomy is often studied by examining the specific body systems, such as the skeletal system, the nervous system, the muscular system, etc. Yet we know that these systems do not work in isolation. In fact, they are totally dependent on one another. Just like the body systems, leadership can be examined by its component parts, even knowing that this is not how it works in real life. We can look at the individual competencies, but we should always remember that without the others, they will fail to function as they should.

As we have mentioned several times already, leadership is interdisciplinary. It can be broken down into two fundamental categories: Leadership Conditions and Leadership Capital. The Conditions have already been examined. If we use the anatomy analogy, the three primary "systems" of Leadership Capital involves an interaction between the leader's philosophy, his personal psychological focus, and his interpersonal interaction with his followers.

We will examine these three primary systems, which each have a complementary pair of competencies. The three are:

- **The philosophical system—vision and values.**

  Everything starts with the philosophical foundation of leaders, represented by their central purpose or vision and their governing values and ideals. The vision of leaders can also be seen as their hope for the future, and the set of values represent a composite of their past.

- **The personal psychological system—wisdom and courage.**

  The internal focus of a leader, the activation of his or her thinking process, comes from the knowledge that has matured into wisdom, which is steadied by courage. Wisdom and courage are guided and influenced by the philosophical system, the leader's vision and values.

- **The interpersonal psychological system—trust and voice.**

  The essential aspect of leadership, which consists of inspiring and influencing others, depends on the relationships that are developed through trust and a consistent voice. The strength of the inspiration and influence is also impacted by the potency of the leader's vision and values.

These six elements of Leadership Capital (the philosophical and psychological determinants) comprise the attributes of a leader. All the thousands of books and articles on leadership can trace the makeup of a leader to these essential characteristics.

Philosophical System = Vision + Values

Everyone has a philosophy toward life. That said, extremely few people are able to put into words that philosophy and even fewer have a consistent philosophy. Leaders who are effective have both vision and values that are in harmony with one another and are also able to clearly articulate and exemplify these to others.

This philosophical system could be called the *worldview* on life. James H. Olthius defines worldview as "the integrative and interpretive framework by which order and disorder are judged, the standard by which reality is managed and pursued. It is the set of hinges on which all our everyday thinking and doing turns."[2] And as Ludwig Wittgenstein aptly penned, "If I want the door to turn, the hinges must stay put."[3]

Like classical philosophy, our worldview answers the big questions of why we are here, where we are going, what is the best way to live, etc. For a leader, these questions are first answered internally in an overall framework that shapes his or her destiny. Then, a leader must fuse this worldview into the operation of his or her organization.

There have been very different organizations like the Jesuits, the U.S. Marine Corps, and Jim Collin's "good to great" business organizations[4] that work the process backward.

The leader is one who has been raised up within the organization and has incorporated its vision and values and continues that legacy.

The vision and values form a framework for all the thinking processes and interactive processes with others that involves the leader. Yet this framework is unseen from the outside; it is an internal compass that guides and directs everything he does. When his personal philosophy is matched to the organization, the effect is often dramatic. Likewise, when the leader's philosophy is mismatched to the organization, or when it is inconsistent, disaster awaits.

A faulty philosophy will play havoc with a leader. I worked with a young entrepreneur who we will call Janis (the Latvian name for John). He had a grand vision for the future. He wanted to develop services that would impact the Baltic nations and beyond to Russia. Janis was a naturally charismatic individual, and his enthusiasm for his vision was contagious to his followers. They followed his lead, worked extremely hard, and in a very short time Janis had built up a company that was quite successful and rapidly expanding.

But Janis was continuously running into problems caused by his inconsistent set of values. I was constantly pointing out these deficiencies and warning him of impending trouble, but he did not see it that way. He felt that his initial success was a sign that he was on the right track. What I saw, however, were confused followers who wondered why the same set of standards did not apply to him as he applied them to others, why some situations were handled ethically and others were not, or why the values he did hold were always changing in priority. I realized that sooner or later, this would spell trouble for Janis.

Janis had a stated set of values; but the reality was that neither he nor his employees knew exactly how he would respond in any given situation. His values were on paper but not in practice. He stated, for example, that his company would always maintain the highest professionalism, and he placed a high emphasis on dressing appropriately, displaying friendly customer service, and quickly handling customer concerns. All of these were important, to be sure, but at a higher level of professionalism involving ethical behavior, he chose to look the other way when it involved one of his top sales people.

Another stated value was openness; he felt open lines of communication were important to the health of an organization. On the surface, there was a level of congeniality within the company. But then he set up a "secret department" to develop a new product but which he did not trust his employees to keep quiet from his competitors. Once, when one of his managers attempted to confront him on some of his weaknesses, Janis became so livid that he called security to throw the manager out of the building.

One by one, his loyal followers became disillusioned and went elsewhere. In the end, his business went bankrupt as Janis squandered all the goodwill created by his vision, not only among his employees, but also his suppliers and customers. In other words, the values ruined the vision. The walk must match the talk.

The goal of transforming a society through a particular product or service must have a corresponding ideal that can make this happen. The philosophy of leaders, their guiding vision and governing values, serve as a reference point for the operation of the personal and interpersonal competencies of wisdom, courage, trust, and voice. When the vision is deficient, then strong values simply make someone a good person. When the values are deficient, then the strong vision will forever be floundering on an inconsistent path.

No one represents a more coherent set of vision and values than Ernest Shackleton on his Endurance Expedition. Every effort in his planning was centered on one single major focus—crossing the Antarctic continent without endangering any lives. Note that this focus had two dimensions—crossing the Antarctic (the vision) with a corresponding value of preservation of life.

The men who followed Shackleton's vision believed in him because of his strong sense of the value of safety. His every action was taken with the idea of what would be best for the men, and they knew it. It was that concern that caused him to turn back on his previous polar expedition when he was within reach of becoming the first man to reach the South Pole. The honor would have most likely cost the life of one of his company, and he chose instead to rescue the crewmember. This is a man who lived his values first, and his vision followed. When the vision to cross the Antarctic was destroyed, he simply set a new vision—to safely return all to England—and moved on. His values endured.

Values come first. James MacGregor Burns, the first real leadership guru, stated that the most essential ingredient for leaders is to have a moral foundation. David Gergen, noted presidential advisor, remarked that the lack of a moral base is the greatest weakness a leader can possess. He noted that research conducted at the Harvard Business School indicates that 85 percent of a leader's performance depends on his or her personal character.[5]

These values are assimilated into every aspect of the organization's operation. Thomas Watson, Jr., former CEO of IBM, observed, "Consider any great organization—one that has lasted over the years—I think you will find it owes its resiliency not to its form of organization or administrative skills, but to the power of what we call beliefs and the appeal these beliefs have for its people."[6] James Collins and Jerry Porras, commenting on this quote in their best-seller, *Built to Last*, noted that Watson was speaking about values.[7]

The great challenge for all leaders is to present a coherent set of vision and values. President Bush has this difficulty with the Global War on Terror. There is almost a universal agreement that militant Islamism has created a danger to much of the Western world. It is Bush's belief that the values of democracy would mute the voice of this extremism and eventually defuse it. By draining the swamps of despotism, the world will be safe. Yet to challenge state-supported terrorism, such as Saddam Hussein's Iraq, means armed force if necessary. In simplest terms, previous American administrations wanted to make the world safe for democracy, but Bush wants democracy to make the world safe.

Many people have a problem with this set of vision and values. They agree that terrorism is a threat, but disagree on the values of democracy and the use of force to implement it as representing the best defense against terrorism. In particular, Western European countries view Bush's values as too "American" for them to support. However, the countries of Eastern Europe that have only recently severed themselves from 50 years of Soviet domination have generally embraced the values and supported President Bush's efforts. This is not the place to argue the merits or weaknesses of President Bush's approach; it is only to illustrate the importance of consistency in a leader's philosophy and how this needs to be effectively presented to the followers in an organization.

A local vision can utilize locally accepted values, but a broader more universal vision needs comparable values. A Baltic firm that has a director, who believes that hiring Baltic citizens rather than other EU nationalities who are more qualified, will doubtless be a locally popular person, but this parochial attitude will not make their brand very popular Europe-wide.

Vision works with values to create the leader's guiding ideology and focus in life. In the Ideal Leadership Model, these two competencies surround the personal and interpersonal attributes of the leader. To continue with the human anatomy analogy, the philosophical system could possibly be compared to the skeletal system. It provides the structure and framework which everything else is built around. A healthy body needs healthy bones!

Personal Characteristics = Wisdom + Courage

If we continue with the human anatomy analogy to Leadership Conditions, we could compare the personal competencies of wisdom and courage to the nervous system of the body. Every action that the body takes is predicated by the nervous system, just as every action of a leader is formed by his or her wisdom and courage.

This personal system in the leader is the resource from which he draws for problem-solving, decision-making, strategic emphasis, allocation of resources, and all the other actions of a leader. Wisdom is knowing what to do; courage is having the will to do it.

From ancient times, wisdom and courage have been seen as two sides of the same coin. Plato believed that were three parts of man; the head represented his intellect and wisdom, his chest represented the will and courage, and the abdomen was where the emotions resided. Though psychology has come a long way in the last couple of thousand years, there is still a strong nugget of truth in that simple illustration.

The Bible has perhaps one of the most profound statements on the conjunction of wisdom and courage of all the early writings. The Book of Proverbs states, *"The fear of the Lord is the beginning of knowledge, but fools despise wisdom and instruction,"* (Prov. 1:7 KJV). Implied in this text is a deep psychological truth—a person cannot grow wiser than that which they fear!

There is a strong symbiotic relationship between learning and wisdom that is inseparably tied to courage. Cognitive psychologists have long known that if a person does not feel that he has at least a 70 percent chance of learning a new idea, he will not expend the mental energy to learn it. In other words, if we are afraid to learn something, we will not be able to. This is why good teachers always try to inspire their students by first building up their confidence. If their fears are not overcome, the best teaching methodologies will be wasted. The heart controls the head, so to speak.

The same thing applies to all areas of a leader's thinking process. The best person I ever hired was an admissions representative for a business school that I worked at. Judy came to the interview dressed in a brilliantly bright red dress that nearly blinded my eyes. This was not the professional attire I expected, and her responses to my questions also were not as polished as I would have preferred them to be. But what I saw in her was a driving willingness to work and to learn. I wanted to take a risk and hire her.

My superior argued with me against doing so, and I realized that if I stuck my neck out and hired Judy against my boss's reservations, I would pay a serious price if she did not work out. Not only did she work out, she ended up replacing me as head of the department when I departed two years later.

But I could have played it safe. I could have gone against my instinctive wisdom out of fear of failure. If I had done so, I would have been practicing less wisdom than I possessed. It follows then, that an individual's strength of mind is determined by his strength of character. The limits of our wisdom are the limits of our fears.

But we all have fears; they are a natural part of man's makeup. Going back to the passage in Proverbs, the Bible states that if man would put his fear up at the highest bar (the fear of God), he would literally have nothing else to be afraid of. As a result, he would be able to act with total wisdom in any situation. History is filled with many great Christian theologians and philosophers as well as leaders who practiced this concept in their lives.

Wisdom is related to problem solving, and this also has its roots in courage. Picture a manager who has just been informed that an employee is late for work again. The manager, Anna, has had problems with Peter for the past six months. He always has a good excuse why he is late, but his work needs to be covered by others, which results in a general backlog in the work process. Anna wants to put a stop to it, so she goes back in her mind to what she has done in the past in similar situations or what she has heard others have done.

This is a typical problem solving methodology—seek to retrieve solutions from past experiences. But the more creative approach is to look at this problem from a fresh point of view. Is there something that could be tried with Peter that has not been tried before? Yes. This might involve more risk, but there is also the possibility that previous experiences are insufficient and perhaps a new, untried idea will be more successful than any previous solution.

This approach can best be seen in Harvard professor Ronald Heifetz's technical/adaptive outlook at leadership issues.[8] Technical problems are similar to management issues; they require routine solutions. However, adaptive problems are ones that require a leader to look at the issue in a different way. This requires courage, because the temptation is simply to respond with a technical solution and move on.

Ernest Shackleton took the man who complained the most about the shortage of food and put him in charge of the supplies. It raised eyebrows all around, but it was a masterstroke. The man was a good steward and he also stopped complaining.

In the case of Anna and the tardy employee Peter, the adaptive answer was to adjust his work schedule. Rather than simply punishing him, which had been tried in the past but failed to rectify the problem, she reworked the system and found it more to everyone's liking. This solution would never have presented itself to Anna if she had simply followed her own previous experience. She was willing to display courage in problem solving, and it led to a greater degree of wisdom.

A person with much wisdom and little courage will accomplish little and probably grow very little in their intellectual abilities. A person with great courage but little wisdom is a dangerous person to be around!

The two competencies are inextricably intertwined. Good leaders grow in their wisdom by having a solid core of courage.

Interpersonal Characteristics = Trust + Voice

If the philosophical competencies are comparable to the skeletal system in the body, and the personal competencies are comparable to the nervous system, then the interpersonal competencies must represent the dermatological system of the body. It is outer skin that we see in a person; and in leaders, the bond of trust they form with their followers and their ability to effectively communicate their message is what others see.

Like the other sets of competencies already considered, these two are also linked together. Without trust, no one listens to the leader. But the reason trust is built is because the leader does and lives what he or she says.

It is this last dimension that truly separates the leader from another person who is simply a nice person to have around. Stephen Covey wrote one of the classic self-help books in 1990, *The Seven Habits of Highly Effective People*. Yet he realized that simply being effective does not produce greatness, so in 2004 he wrote another book, *The Eighth Habit: From Effectiveness to Greatness*. And what is the eighth habit? Finding your voice and inspiring others to find theirs through developing trust relationships.

A man or woman might have the philosophical and personal systems in abundance, but until they display them in the interpersonal dimension, these systems remain hidden "under the skin" so to speak. No one illustrates this better than President Harry S Truman.

Truman was selected as the Vice President for President Franklin Roosevelt's fourth term of office in 1944. No one expected much of this anonymous and diminutive man from the Midwest because Roosevelt's three previous vice presidents had been largely figureheads. The vice president would assume the presidency if the president died, of course, but this was far from everyone's mind because an American president had not died in office since President McKinley's assassination a half century before. But just a few months after his fourth inauguration, President

Roosevelt suffered a stroke and died in April 1945. After nearly 13 years in office, the leader who had led the United States through the Great Depression and into World War II was gone. The unknown, untried, and unassuming Harry S. Truman had inherited the mantle of head of government of the most powerful country in the world.

But there was strength in this little man, and he displayed it immediately. One cabinet official was notified that he would be handing in his resignation, and when the official asked if the president had made that decision before he died, Truman replied, "No, the president made that decision just now."

Harry Truman constantly was under the shadow of his predecessor, but he never let it stop him from doing what he needed to do. He slowly built a base of support that was not just to the office of the presidency, but also to him personally. His strength was in his ability to simply speak the truth. He was once quoted in *Look* magazine as saying, "I never give them hell. I just tell the truth, and they think it is hell."

He practiced that same straightforward approach when forced to make incredibly difficult decisions like the dropping of the atomic bomb on Japan and relieving from command the popular General Douglas MacArthur during the Korean War. When a decision needed to be made—he made it. Though this earned him more than his share of enemies, he was still able to win an election in his own right in 1948.

Harry Truman realized that he was not Franklin D. Roosevelt, nor could he ever be. He had to display his own voice or "story"—the straight-thinking, plain-speaking Harry Truman. It took time for the people of the United States to adapt to their new leader, especially because the previous one was such a legend, but it eventually happened. The trust was joined to the voice, and Truman is recognized today as one of America's great presidents.

Growing and Going

An individual must focus on what he has control over, and not what he does not have control over. Leadership conditions, for the most part, lie outside of the control of most of us. At best, we have indirect control over these conditions. (One Swedish professor, however, related a story to me of a class he was teaching as guest lecturer for a group of high school students. When he mentioned that no one could be sure exactly of what they would do when they grew up, the class began to giggle. When he asked what was so funny, one girl remarked that she was sure of what she was going to do. That student turned out to be Crown Princess Victoria.)

Unless we have royal blood or other advantages, however, conditions must be anticipated and not contrived. Rather, it is Leadership Capital that should be our focus. Imagine leadership represented by two concentric circles. The inner circle represents Leadership Capital. It is the essence of leadership. This is what the leader and potential leader can recognize and develop in themselves and others. As Stephen Covey explains, this inner circle can be thought of as the circle of control.[9] It represents what the leader can actually determine and expand. It is in this crucible that the leader's potential can be developed.

The outer circle of leadership is Leadership Conditions. This circle shows areas that impact the leader's ability to lead, which include the conditions and environment in which they are working. This area is the circle of concern. The leader does not, in large part, determine it. Leaders circumstantially find themselves having to make the best of whatever situation they find themselves in. Some succeed and some do not. The only difference between a diamond and a piece of coal is that a diamond was able to hold its ground under pressure for a longer period of time.

Leadership is an organic concept, which means that the individual parts can be examined, but it is only when they all are present and congruent with one another that the real synergy of leadership takes place. In saying this, however, not all the elements are equally important to each leader. Research done at the Stockholm School of Economics in Riga has shown that as the size of domain of an organization grows, different areas of Leadership Capital presence become more important. At the very beginning of growth, trust is most important. Usually small organizations are grouped around the personality and strength of a leader. In these earliest stages, a leader generally chooses individuals to work with primarily based on his or her ability to trust them.

As an organization begins to grow larger, however, it becomes more important to apply leadership wisdom. This is when a company finds itself suffering with "growing pains" and needs to structure itself better. As an organization grows from medium to large size, voice becomes preeminent. Many organizations of this size complain about the flow of information and how it is managed. The leader needs to maintain a clear voice during this time to keep all the noses pointed in the same direction. Finally, as an organization reaches maximum size, courage becomes most important. At this stage, failures can be catastrophic.

In leadership literature, there is an advocate or "champion" for every one of the specific leadership competencies. Winston Churchill, for example, felt that courage is the most important element of leadership. Warren Bennis, one of the leading writers in the leadership genre, states that trust is the essence of leadership. Warren Buffett, probably the most successful investor of the 20th century, believes that vision is the key to leadership. As was mentioned earlier, one of the first great leadership writers, James MacGregor Burns, argues that values are the most important.

A leader should have, of course, all attributes in operation at every stage or phase of an organization's growth. But the "anatomy" of Leadership Capital presence demonstrates that developing Leadership Capital must never stop during a leader's life. At every stage, at every age, leaders must continually assess themselves and their progress in developing their Leadership *Capital*. When *Conditions* are right, the leader makes his or her move. That is the essential aspect which will be considered next.

THE LEADER'S PRAYER

God, grant me the serenity to accept what cannot be changed, give me the courage to change what should be changed, and give me the wisdom to distinguish one from another.

Reinhold Niebuhr

Endnotes

1. Lansing, Alfred. *Endurance: Shackleton's Incredible Voyage* (Carroll & Graf, New York, NY, 1999), Alexander, Caroline. *The Endurance: Shackleton's Legendary Antarctic Expedition* (Alfred A. Knopf, New York, NY, 1998) and Morell, Margot. *Shackleton's Way: Leadership Lessons from the Great Antarctic Explorer* (Penguin, New York, NY, 2002) are probably the best books on the subject; and NOVA and A&E have produced excellent film versions as well.

2. Olthius, James. H., "On Worldviews" *Christian Scholars Review*, (Volume XIV, Number 2, 1985), 153.

3. Wittgenstein, Ludwig. *On Certainty* (Harper Torchbooks, New York, NY, 1969).

4. Collins, Jim. *Good to Great: Why Some Companies Make the Leap and Why Some Don't* (HarperCollins, New York, NY, 2001). These companies include Abbott Laboratories, Kroger, Nucor, Philip Morris, Pitney Bowes, Walgreens, Gillette, Wells Fargo, Fannie Mae, Kimberly Clark, and Circuit City.

5. Gergen, David. Spoken at the *Leadership in the 21st Century Forum*, Kennedy School of Government, Harvard University (Cambridge, MA, December 2003).

6. Watson, Thomas Jr. *A Business and Its Beliefs: The Ideas that Helped Build IBM* (McGraw-Hill, 1962).

7. Collins, Jim. *Built to Last: Successful Habits of Visionary Companies* (HarperCollins, New York, NY, 2002).

8. Heifetz, Ronald A. *Leadership Without Easy Answers* (Belknap Press, Cambridge, MA, 1994).

9. Covey, Stephen. *The Seven Habits of Highly Effective People* (Simon & Schuster, New York, NY, 1989).

Key Ideas

1. Capital is the personal and interpersonal characteristics that make up a leader's presence, combined with the leader's philosophical framework. Like the body systems, these various competencies can be studied separately, but they work congruently in a leader's life.

2. The leader's philosophical framework is formed by his vision and values. It provides the direction he wishes to move in and the road or means used to fulfill it.

3. The leader's personal perspective is developed from his wisdom and courage. Courage opens up the window for sound wisdom in solving problems and making decisions.

4. The leader's interpersonal interaction is his trust and voice. Trust binds the followers to the leader, and voice is the "story" or message he represents.

5. While all competencies are equally important, they are not all equally important at all times in the leader's experience.

Questions for Active Leaders

1. Imagine you have 50 units of "leadership" that could be attributed to any proportion to your own Leadership Capital competencies (e.g., 20 units for values, 10 units for courage, 15 units for trust, and 5 units for voice). In what areas would you most like to improve?

2. In leadership literature, there is an advocate or "champion" for every one of the specific leadership competencies. Winston Churchill, for example, felt that courage is the most important element of leadership. Which competency would you most like to represent you?

Questions for FLOWters (Future Leaders of the World)

1. Read a biographical sketch of any leader and seek to identify the six competencies that he or she possesses.

2. Read and memorize the Leader's Prayer. What part do you believe represents the greatest challenge for you?

CHAPTER SEVEN

The Fifth Essential—
The Magic of Connection

Eve of Destruction or Opportunity?

The American Civil War was a defining moment not only in American history, but world history as well. Had the southern Confederate states been successful in their attempt at succession, the world would truly have been a different place. The southern states initially enjoyed great success under their brilliant commander, Robert E. Lee. For the first two years, he never suffered a major defeat on the field of battle. Then, in June 1863, Lee boldly marched his army northward into Pennsylvania. He believed that if he could engage and defeat the northern army on its own territory, President Lincoln would have no choice but to sue for peace.

The armies coincidentally converged on the small crossroads town of Gettysburg in southern Pennsylvania. General Lee had many advantages in his favor, not the least of which were troops who were fiercely loyal to him. The northern Union Army had just changed commanders (again), and newly appointed General Meade knew that his troops were demoralized and tired. It would be a tough battle.

Marching toward Gettysburg for the Union was a small detachment, the 20th Maine, under the command of Colonel Joshua Chamberlain. A professor of rhetoric at Bowdein College before the war, Chamberlain himself had just been recently promoted to serve as leader of his band of a little less than 300 troops. On the eve before the first day of battle, Chamberlain was informed that he was being given custody of approximately 100 "mutineers" from another Maine regiment. These men had grown weary of the mismanagement they had seen from their commanders, and when their unit was being disbanded and the members reassigned, they simply refused. They decided they were done fighting.

Colonel Chamberlain was in an impossible situation. He could not afford to divert attention from the impending conflict to guard these men. He had been given permission to shoot them if required, but felt that this was not a viable option either. What he really needed was for the men to pick up their arms again and fight. So he made an impassioned speech, and eventually all but six of the entire group agreed to voluntarily join his unit.

This event would barely merit a footnote had it not been for the heroic actions of the 20th Maine in the Battle of Gettysburg. Against overwhelming odds, they were able to hold the left flank of the Union army's line at Little Round Top. Many men died, and nearly all of them were wounded in the action, including Chamberlain himself. Had they not had those additional one hundred men, there is no way they could have held off the enemy.

Because they held, the Confederates lost their advantage and eventually lost the battle. For his efforts, Colonel Chamberlain was awarded the nation's highest military decoration, the Medal of Honor.

But as important as his efforts on the field of battle, his speech to the mutineers was almost as significant. His ability to persuade those men to pick up their arms was the key to holding Little Round Top. It was a "magic moment"—the kind that makes or breaks leaders.

Good GOLI's Make Great Leaders

The fifth leadership essential states that, **Success in leadership happens when Conditions and Capital coincide**. Joshua Chamberlain was faced with a pivotal moment—the coinciding of Conditions with a man whose Leadership Capital was precisely needed for that moment. He could not lead men who would not follow, but if he could persuade them, it would give him a definite advantage in the upcoming battle. As a professor of rhetoric, Chamberlain understood the dynamics of effective speech. Beyond that, he also knew the type of men he was leading. The opportunity came and he grabbed it.

Larry Greiner wrote an article for *Harvard Business Review* in 1972 that has since become holy writ in business vernacular—the concept of the organizational life cycle. Just as people and products have a limited life cycle, so does any organization have a certain point where it peaks and then begins to descend. This idea in and of itself is not particularly groundbreaking, but Greiner's genius was to note that there are several demarcation points all along the organization's path, which represent turning points. In other words, every organization faces crossroads where it is either renewing itself or beginning to die. As Franklin Roosevelt so eloquently said, "We are either living out a new vision or the death of an old one."

Greiner termed these pivotal moments "periods of revolution" because they typically exhibit a serious upheaval of management practices. He states, "Traditional management practices that were appropriate for a smaller size and earlier time no longer work and are brought under scrutiny by frustrated top-level managers and disillusioned lower level managers. During such periods of crisis, a number of companies fall short. Those that are unable to abandon past practices and effect major organizational changes are likely either to fold or to level off in their growth rates."[1]

The people who take charge of these opportunities have been called "rifters" by one expert.[2] He notes that a tear in the fabric of the normal course of events creates a rift, which opportunists like Walt Disney, Steve Jobs, and others are bold and creative enough to jump on and use to their advantage. Maxwell House had the positioning to create coffee shops around the nation, but did not see the rift, or chose to ignore it. Whereas Howard Schultz, the chairman and chief global strategist of Starbucks, did see the rift and took advantage of it.

We choose to call these intersections on the road of organizational development GOLI's or Gateways of Leadership Initiative. A leader who recognizes such a moment has opportunity for a good GOLI (pronounced "golly").

If he or she fails to take the initiative or makes a mistake in using it, this is termed a FOLI—a Failure of Leadership Initiative. No leader has a perfect record of GOLI's, but a string of FOLI's will definitely limit one's effectiveness and probably result in dismissal from a leadership position.

GOLI's may present themselves at any time. The fifth essential says that success in leadership happens when Conditions and Capital coincide. Remember that the Conditions constitute the period, people, place, or position in which the leader finds himself or herself.

A GOLI may happen because the **period** is opportune:

- A new feature for a product or service is developed.
- A new market niche opens up.
- A competitor changes strategy.
- A financial windfall occurs.
- A government incentive is offered.
- A new technological advance is made.

A GOLI may happen because the **people** are more responsive:

- Employees display greater proficiency.
- Expansion attracts new employees with new enthusiasm.
- A difficult employee departs, creating a fresh atmosphere.
- Employees express interest in being delegated new tasks.

A GOLI may happen because the **position** or **place** of the leader has changed:

- The leader is assigned a new position of increased responsibility.
- The leader gains new insights and wants to test them out.
- The leader aligns with others who strengthen his leadership capabilities.

In all of these, a director or decision-maker within the organization can choose to do nothing—simply continue with business as usual. None of these developments force the leader to act. Yet a failure to do so may mark a demarcation spot where decline begins due to a missed opportunity for growth and development.

All of the above are what might be termed opportunities for a GOLI. There are other situations where the leader does not have a choice—the GOLI is thrust upon them:

- The *period* is one of financial instability, inflation, depression, or other negative economic conditions.

- The *people* have done something unethical or unprofessional which causes a negative image upon the organization.

- The *position* or *place* of the leader has changed, and he is no longer capable of influencing a change or as much of a change within the organization.

These negative GOLI's appear at first to be a disaster. Nature teaches us this lesson from time to time. In an area near the Grand Canyon in the United States, the Forest Service had tried to plant pine trees for decades without success. Then a massive fire occurred in the area that thinned out the brush; the heat opened the cones in surrounding trees, which caused the seeds to fall and sprout. Today there is a thriving pine forest in that area. A leader's vision helps him or her to see something good when the smoke is rising in the trees.

A Russian friend of mine who delivers motivational talks believes in this principle to such a degree that he wrote a book in Russian on the subject, *I Love Trouble*. When setbacks are viewed, not as obstacles, but opportunities for leadership initiative, good things can often result. The best example of this was the Marine Corps commander in the Korean War who was informed that his unit was completely surrounded. "Good," he responded, "Now we can shoot in any direction and hit someone."

The Christian faith offers a useful illustration of the GOLI/FOLI principle. Evangelical Christianity states that while an individual is offered a free gift of salvation, he or she subsequently grows in his or her faith by aspiring toward Jesus' example of life. According to the Book of James in the Bible, problems are allowed to arise in the Christian's life for the sole purpose of serving as a catalyst to this growth. When problems arise in his or her path, the Christian is forced to choose whether to take a high road of deeper conviction, or choose the lower road of compromise of faith. The difficulties actually serve as a vehicle for spiritual growth.

Organizations, as well as people, must face growth pains. Greiner notes that the transitional states take place at key stages of organizational development. Research conducted on the Ideal Leadership Model (as mentioned in the previous chapter) has revealed that certain competencies are more critical during these particular stages. Combining Greiner's model with Ideal Leadership, we can identify four key developmental stages that correspond to a particular leadership competency. We could term these the Trust Stage, the Wisdom Stage, the Voice Stage, and the Courage Stage.

The Trust Stage = The Infant and Pioneer Organization

Start-up companies are often vibrant, exciting, and alive. There is an entrepreneur with a novel idea that is being implemented into some product or service. A small band of assistants, who often must wear a number of different hats, assist the entrepreneur in this endeavor. Rules are usually at a minimum at this stage, as well as the compensation expected. The hours are long, the problems are legion, but there is a sense that all of this dedication will pay off in the end.

At this stage of an organization, everything is based on trust. The workers are willing to give much more than they are being adequately compensated for, on the basis that they will share in the future success of the company. Suppliers who serve this type of organization also must act in faith, as the company has no track record to show its good faith as a customer. The customers and clients of the organization must also have a high degree of trust, because there is not much more than an idea that they are buying. The brand has not been established, so the trust goes back to the leader himself.

Most of the GOLI's at this stage are related to trust. This was what Colonel Chamberlain had to establish before he could begin to lead his men into battle. He needed their trust, and so he asked for it. The 1993 film *Gettysburg* portrays the scene very vividly. When Chamberlain is given command of the mutineers, he is told by the officer handing them over that these men could be shot for insubordination. "You want to shoot them, Colonel, shoot them. No one would say nothing about it." Chamberlain diplomatically rebukes him by ignoring his statement and dismissing him, and does so in front of the men. When he first meets the men, he immediately asks about their well-being. One of the mutineers, Private Buckley, acts as a spokesperson and asks to meet with Chamberlain privately. Chamberlain listens with respect, and then addresses the concerns Buckley raises when he speaks to the men directly.

All of Chamberlain's actions were designed to build trust. In a small organization, everything is related to the trust of the leader. The followers are not joined to an organization as much as they are to a builder's dream. They trust that this dream will succeed. Suppliers and clients are also acting on trust that the leader can fulfill what he or she has promised.

They may fail to see the dream materialize, which means the organization will fade away into the night like so many others. In the early 1990s, Rusty Shaffer had an idea to design a guitar to teach beginners how to play. He designed a guitar, which had a rotary dial on the body of the guitar used to select a scale or chord in a particular key. When powered up, LEDs set in the fretboard would glow under the appropriate string and fret to show you where to put your fingers for the scale or chord selected with the rotary switch. It was a novel idea and had lots of promise, but despite putting enormous time and energy into the project, he finally accepted defeat. His product simply did not live up to expectations.

But ten years later, Shaffer recognized that technology had progressed to the point where he should try again. This time, his Optek Fretlight Guitar was a stunning success. By integrating computer software with the guitar, the new generation Fretlight offered thousands more options than the old rotary dial. Plus, LED technology had also progressed to the degree that the lights on the frets were virtually invisible when not lit up.

It is a fantastic product and Optek has been receiving rave reviews from many major journals and media outlets.[3]

Rusty Shaffer faced a GOLI and did not succeed initially because his product was not ready. He could not create the trust in its performance that he envisioned. This is a common problem with inventors, designers, and entrepreneurs. They see what they want to build very clearly in their minds, but making it concrete is often a different story. Shaffer failed, but then waited for another GOLI, and this time succeeded.

Every GOLI the leader faces at these embryonic stages of the organization's development somehow impact the trust factor. A good leader will recognize this when facing these challenges, and will always make the choice that will increase—not decrease—the trust from others.

The Wisdom Stage = The Rational Organization

I enjoyed the Leadership School I attended during the 1980s. It consisted of monthly meetings held at Perkin's Pancake House, immediately after our regular school board meeting ended. The five or six school board members who would not have to rush home to their wives would enjoy sitting over a cup of coffee and discussing a wide range of issues far into the night. Some of the finest leaders I ever had the opportunity to know were in that group.

One night we were discussing a donation that a local church had received of one million dollars. One man simply dropped a million bucks on the pastor after church one Sunday. We fantasized all the things we could do for our school if such a windfall would fall our way. We imagined building improvements, teacher salary increases, new program offerings, field trips for students to faraway places, and many other great ideas. But after we were done brainstorming, we backtracked and thought about the ramifications of each of those ideas.

Any building improvement would have to be maintained, as well as any program or equipment acquisition. Teachers might expect similar increases in subsequent years. Parents who currently volunteered would probably expect to be paid. On and on we reflected, and finally we concluded that it was a good thing that no one had donated a million dollars to us!

This simple story illustrates the GOLI that opens up when an organization begins to grow and expand, especially when it happens suddenly. Greiner notes, "The critical task for management in each revolutionary period is to find a new set of organizational practices that will become the basis for managing the next period of evolutionary growth. Interestingly enough, those new practices eventually sow the seeds of their own decay and lead to another period of revolution. Managers therefore experience the irony of seeing a major solution in one period become a major problem in a later period."[4]

This creates difficulty at every stage, but it is especially crucial for the organization that has outgrown its infancy and is now what is termed a "rational" company. At this stage, it has an established customer base, standardized operations for most practices, and is on more or less solid financial footing. Most importantly, it generally has had to expand its personnel beyond those whose chief attribute was their loyalty to the founder. Now there are managers who are focused on the production and improvement of the actual product and service itself. They are not dreamers; they are doers.

Most small-to-medium businesses fall into this category. In normal day-to-day operations, they fare well. But as we noted earlier, life is never status quo for long. Sooner or later, something will happen that will necessitate a change. There will either be a great opportunity that is too good to let go by, or a crisis will arise that will impact the future of the organization. In either case, leadership is needed to make the GOLI a good one.

Very few people outside of the northeastern United States have ever heard of Stroehmann Bread, and the reason is because of the company's history of missed GOLI's. With different decisions, they could be one of the largest producers of bread in the world today.

The company was started by Frederick G. Stroehmann who learned the baking trade as a youth in Germany. At age 16, he immigrated to Wheeling, West Virginia, where he got a job in a small, local bakery. Five years later, he married the owner's daughter, and in 1892 took over the family business, producing and selling under the label, "Mothers Made Bread."

From the beginning he took pride in baking bread the old-fashioned "Pennsylvania Dutch" way with nutritious good taste. The Stroehmann family of three girls and two boys lived in a small apartment over the bakery. They delivered their fresh-baked bread by horse and carriage, and soon the business began to prosper.

In 1918, Frederick built a new bakery in Huntingdon, West Virginia, and with the breakout of World War I, began supplying bread to an Army training camp. The demand soon exceeded the bakery's capacity, and a third bakery in Ashland, Kentucky, was purchased. Both bakeries were kept busy around-the-clock, and by the end of the war, Stroehmann had become a household name.

At this point, Stroehmann's was positioned to dominate the bread-making market in America. But instead, in 1922, Frederick sold his three bakeries to Mr. W.B. Ward of United Bakeries. The "Mothers Made" label was changed to "Wonder Bread," and the three bakeries became the Continental Baking Company. Today, Continental has 40 bakeries throughout the U.S., and Wonder Bread is the best-selling brand of bread sold.

But that was all in the future. Two years after their father liquidated the company, his two sons, Carl and Harold J. decided to get into the bakery business themselves. They purchased the Gramlich Bakery in Williamsport, Pennsylvania, and renamed it "Stroehmann Brothers Company." The brothers built a successful business based on their father's principle of providing a quality product at a fair price. In 1927, they purchased a plant in Norristown, Pennsylvania, and produced a radically new product—sliced white bread. They introduced it with strong advertising, and soon Stroehmann was the most popular brand in the marketplace.

Successful GOLI's followed the brothers as acquisitions and new plant openings continued through the years. In 1955, Harold J. Stroehmann, Jr. took over the company. To promote Stroehmann's commitment to its old-fashioned baking ideals of freshness, good taste, and good nutrition, the company created the famous "Grampa Stroehmann" character. "Grampa" appeared on many of the company's baked goods products, and became the official registered trademark for Stroehmann Brothers Company.

For the second time, it appeared that Stroehmann's was strategically placed to dominate the bread market, but then in 1977, Harold Stroehmann died. His older brother Carl, who was well on in years by this time, had been serving as the chairman of the board of directors in much of a figurehead position while his brother had run all the company's operations. Carl had a GOLI—he could and should have used the opportunity to bring in someone with the wisdom to take Stroehmann's to a higher level. Instead, the elderly gentleman tried to implement his wisdom back into the company. The results were nearly disastrous. It would take another decade before Stroehmann's eventually began to turn a corner and build again, but by then they had missed the GOLI. They were eventually bought out by the George Weston Bakeries family.

Wisdom is critically needed to move an organization forward, especially one that is successful at one stage but has the potential to rise higher. In many cases, this wisdom does not reside within the same entrepreneur who initially developed the organization in the first place. It takes strong leaders to have strong people around them to make them wiser.

The Voice Stage = The Established Organization

I once saw a cross-country ski race in Sweden that included over 30,000 racers. By the time the racers in the back of the group were able to start, the ones in the front were almost finished! Many large organizations suffer with the same problem. By the time the people at the bottom of the chain get the message, the ones at the top are off in some new direction. The most difficult task for any large organization spread out nationally and internationally, is to keep everyone focused in the same direction.

People Express Airlines is a boom-to-bust story that exemplifies a FOLI due to a lack of voice. Founded by Don Burr, the low-cost air travel carrier, People Express began operations out of Newark Airport on April 30, 1981.

Immediately successful, the company rapidly added more routes, and by May 1983, they offered nonstop service from Newark to London's Gatwick airport. Flights were priced at $149 each way and upon launch, became an instant success with all flights sold out for several months within 24 hours of being offered.

Don Burr was riding high (no pun intended), and decided that acquisition would be a logical move to expand his success. In 1985, People Express bought out Denver-based Frontier Airlines. The combined company became the United States' fifth largest airline, with flights to most major U.S. cities, as well as an additional transatlantic route to Brussels. People Express also purchased Britt Airways and Provincetown-Boston Airlines (PBA) during this period, both small carriers with routes in the Midwest, Northeast, and Florida.

This was a calculated GOLI, to be sure, and if all these new companies had shared in the frugal economy mind-set of People Express, it might just have worked. But a clear voice was not forthcoming. Instead, Frontier's labor force resisted, and the passengers were also not pleased with the change to a low-fare, no-frills mentality. If this was not bad enough for People Express, it was also facing new challenges from competitors who were beginning to match its fares.

A stronger voice at the pivotal time of transition could have made the difference. The alignment of the new airlines could have produced a bold new company that would have developed new strategies and possibly become the major air carrier in the United States. But it was not to be. People Express crash-landed. They ceased to exist as a carrier on February 1, 1987, when its routes and assets were merged into the operations of Continental Airlines.

Strong leaders have a strong voice, and that voice is never more needed than when an organization seems to be growing in all different directions at once. Contrast People Express with another similar low-cost, no-frills carrier, Southwest Airlines. Because it was passenger airliners that were hijacked for the terrorist acts committed against the United States on September 11, 2001, the impact of that event affected the airline industry worst of all. But Southwest knew how to survive—they had been doing it for decades.

The company began operations after overcoming many initial road-blocks in June 1971. From the beginning, Southwest had a simple strategy; fly primarily short-haul (less than 500 miles), point-to-point flights, use a fleet consisting only of Boeing 737s, operate high-frequency flights, offer low fares, and have no international flights They were unique in that they operated without major hubs, which meant that planes were not waiting on the ground for passengers from connecting flights. Their average turnaround time was 15 minutes compared to the industry average of 45 minutes. Customers received no frills, but they were rewarded with the lowest cost of seat mile in the industry. And Southwest also had the best safety record in the airline business. Southwest has ranked number one in fewest customer complaints for the last 11 consecutive years as published in the Department of Transportation's Air Travel Consumer Report.[5]

This formula had enormous advantages that resulted in great profitability. Southwest bucked the airline industry trend of declining profits by posting a profit for 29 consecutive years, averaging more than 12 percent annual return on investment.

Southwest ranked second among companies across all industry groups, and first in the airline industry, in *Fortune* magazine's 2002 list of America's Most Admired Companies.

What made all this work was the presence of Herb Kelleher, CEO of Southwest from 1981 to 2001. His leadership style could best be described as maverick. He played Big Daddy-O in one of the company's videos, appeared as Elvis Presley in in-flight magazine advertisements, and earned the nickname the "High Priest of Ha-Ha" from *Fortune* magazine.[6] But he was not just fun and games. At one point he froze his salary for five years in response to pilots agreeing to do the same. Often when he flew, he would help the ground crew unload bags or help the flight crew serve drinks. His ability to remember names and family details was legendary. He lived out the meaning of customer service and profession-alism, but with a flair for fun, that created great *esprit-de-corps* among the employees and the lowest turnover among workers in the industry.

This is why the GOLI of September 11 that nearly drove the rest of the airline industry into bankruptcy barely made a nick in Southwest's bal-ance sheet. According to the Southwest 2001 annual report, "Southwest was well poised, financially, to withstand the potentially devastating hammer blow of September 11. Why? Because for several decades our leadership philosophy has been: we manage in good times so that our company and our People can be job secure and prosper through bad times....Once again, after September 11, our philosophy of managing in good times so as to do well in bad times proved a marvelous prophylac-tic for our Employees and our Shareholders."

The Courage Stage = The Transforming Organization

Anyone who writes and lectures on the subject of leadership is often asked whom they consider the greatest leader of all. I generally answer by sharing who I believe was the greatest leader of the 20th century— Winston Churchill. Few men in history have embodied the six leader-ship competencies as comprehensively as this man—and it was never needed as much as when he lived.

At one time Great Britain was an empire on which the sun never set, but by the 1930s, those days were long gone. World War I had severely crippled the country, and she was struggling like the rest of the world through a Great Depression. When Britain was forced to intervene against Nazi aggression on the European continent, she was soundly defeated. From May 26 until June 3, 1940, Britain was forced to evacuate some 385,000 troops, including more than 100,000 Frenchmen, using just seven hundred small crafts with brave captains.

It was a humiliating disaster. The German conquest of France was complete. Germany held the Benelux countries. All of Europe lay open before the Nazis. What could Great Britain hope to do? Winston

Churchill had been serving as Prime Minister for less than a month. Everyone, all the way up to the King himself, expected Churchill to sue for peace with Nazi Germany. There seemed to be no other option.

But Winston Churchill was cut from a different cloth than others. A student of history, he may have remembered the ancient Greek battle where the Laconians were trapped on the shore with their backs to a cliff.

The Armada commander sent in a message: "Surrender unconditionally. If we take you by force, we will slaughter you and your male children after we have raped your wives and daughters in front of you." The Laconians responded with a single word, "If."

When Winston Churchill went before the House of Commons to deliver his address, he electrified the nation. "We shall fight on the seas and oceans, we shall fight with growing confidence and growing strength in the air, we shall defend our Island, whatever the cost may be, we shall fight on the beaches, we shall fight on the landing grounds, we shall fight in the fields and in the streets, we shall fight in the hills; we shall never surrender." And with Winston Churchill as their leader—they never did.

Nothing is more difficult than turning around an organization that believes it is at the end. The transforming process begins with a leader who can articulate and demonstrate courage. Churchill's presence was everywhere during the Battle of Britain, his famous "V" for victory sign a constant reminder that he believed the Allies would eventually prevail.

Being a leader of a great nation is always difficult, and Great Britain has not always had leaders at the helm when faced with crises such as those with the Jews of Palestine, the Turkish Cypriots, the Irish of Northern Ireland, or the white settlers of Rhodesia. The solution was generally to ignore the problem. So when the Argentine military seized the Falkland Islands in 1982, no one expected much to come of it. But the Argentines miscalculated—there was an Iron Lady living at 10 Downing Street.

Her name was Margaret Thatcher, and though there was no public passion to reclaim the islands, Maggie knew that there was more at stake to these remote islands than some interest in maintaining old colonial conquests. Great Britain had been conducting negotiations with Argentina for the past 17 years, and was willing to consent to the change of sovereignty. But the 1,800 inhabitants were all English speaking "Kelpers," and every referendum showed that they preferred British rule, even when the British themselves prodded them otherwise.

The action of Argentina, therefore, was a naked power grab, and to Thatcher's way of thinking, an affront to democracy itself. It would not go unchallenged. The result was the sole example of a major naval and amphibious operation between modern forces since the Second World War, ending in a British victory and a collapse of the Argentine government.

To conduct a major military engagement 8,000 miles away, especially given that the issue itself was not one that would directly impact the average British citizen, took tremendous courage on the part of Margaret Thatcher. It is a remarkable and rare thing—courage. But when it comes to transformation of an organization, it is a necessity.

A leader never knows when his or her moment of opportunity will come. They should always be aware, however, that it *will* come. Ann Landers' often-quoted saying is quite true, "Opportunities are usually disguised as hard work, so most people don't recognize them." Good leaders do—and act—and make a difference!

THE LEADER'S REFLECTION

I returned, and saw under the sun, that the race is not to the swift, nor the battle to the strong, neither yet bread to the wise, nor yet riches to men of understanding, nor yet favor to men of skill; but time and chance happened to them all.

(The Bible, Ecclesiastes 9:11 KJV)

Endnotes

1. Greiner, Larry. "Evolution and Revolution as Organizations Grow" *Harvard Business Review*, (Jul/Aug 1972), 37-46.

2. Godin, Seth. "The Secret of Rifting" *Fast Company*, March 2000.

3. Information gleaned from the company website: http://www.optekmusic.com/newhome.htm.

4. Greiner, 40.

5. The Air Travel Consumer Report is a monthly product of the Department of Transportation's Office of Aviation Enforcement and Proceedings. The report is designed to assist consumers with information on the quality of services provided by the airlines. See http://airconsumer.ost.dot.gov/reports/atcr03.htm.

6. Labich, Kenneth. "Is Herb Kelleher America's Best CEO?" *Fortune*, (May 2, 1994), 44-52.

Key Ideas

1. Success in leadership happens when the Leadership Conditions and Capital coincide.

2. These "leadership moments" are precipitated by some change that has taken place in the conditions: the people, place, position, or period.

3. When this moment is used in an advantageous way, using good Leadership Capital, it becomes a "Gateway to Leadership Initiative" or GOLI.

4. When the leader fails to take advantage of the leadership moment, it becomes a "Failure of Leadership Initiative" or FOLI.

5. The four stages of organizational development correspond to the need for Leadership Capital; for the infant and pioneer organization trust is critical, the rational organization needs a leader with wisdom, voice is essential for the established organization and the transforming organization requires a leader with courage.

Questions for Active Leaders

1. At what stage do you see your organization right now? Do you believe that the leadership competency you possess at this stage is appropriate for the moment?

2. What GOLI are you most proud of? What made it so for you?

Questions for FLOWters (Future Leaders of the World)

1. The GOLI/FOLI concept is very helpful in analyzing leadership cases. Read the story of any organizational change and try to pinpoint the characteristics of a leadership moment.

2. Can you identify a turning point in your life up to this point? What aspect of the Leadership Conditions could this turning point be attributed to?

CHAPTER EIGHT

The Sixth Essential—
The Misfortune of Collapse

Behold the Anti-Leader

I once had a conversation with a high-ranking Latvian government official who was complaining about the difficulties of balancing the need for an open market with the need to protect the public and local interests from those who would take advantage of them. I sympathized with his predicament, but told him he could not have it both ways. I compared the societies of the former Soviet republics with a room that had had all the doors and windows sealed shut. The air in such a room was dead and lifeless. Once the windows were opened, however, fresh air rushed in and provided welcome refreshment from the former stale atmosphere. But along with the air from an open window came flies and other pests that had previously been kept out. I told the official, "Sorry, but when the window is thrown open, you are going to get the bad with the good."

So it is with leadership. Leadership Conditions are the catalysts to leadership, and those with strong Leadership Capital can take advantage of those Conditions to make their organizations stronger with wholesome principles and a captivating vision of progress. This is the essence behind the *Ideal* or *Interdisciplinary Leadership Model*. However, those Conditions do not serve as a filter. At the other extreme of the spectrum are those who use their position of power for vainglory pursuit of selfish gain. They must also be considered when discussing leadership. These are the type whom we identify as *anti-leaders*.

Anti-leaders are those who serve in a leadership capacity who do not necessarily possess Leadership Capital as it has been defined here. They find themselves in authority over others because the Conditions worked out for them. As has been stated, it is the Leadership Conditions that serve as the catalyst to individuals finding themselves able to serve. But the conditions can happen *before* an individual is ready or has the capacity or capability to serve.

The sixth leadership essential is **failure in leadership is a result of changing Conditions or misapplied Capital**. As we noted in the last chapter, failure might not be willful but simply a missed GOLI. But a more serious condition exists when those, who purposely capitalize on favorable conditions to assume a place of leadership, do not use, possess, or have not developed the Leadership Capital necessary to effectively move their organization forward in a positive direction.

Even the best leaders have, from time to time, displayed anti-leader tendencies. Whenever leaders place their own good and welfare before the organization and people they serve, they are walking down the path of anti-leadership.

Adolph Hitler would have to be the prototype anti-leader. Many have wondered how this Austrian-born corporal in the German army with a seemingly modest intellect and virtually no social skills could have become one of the century's greatest figures. The answer is that he was a man who was able to capitalize on the Conditions of leadership.

When Hitler joined the Nazi Party in September 1919 at the age of 30, it was called the German Workers' Party. At this time, the party was quite small and ineffective. It was still uncertain of its aims and divided in leadership, but committed to a program of nationalist and socialist principles. There was a leadership vacuum, and Hitler was able to take advantage and fill the void.

Hitler had a certain gift for manipulation, so he put all his energy into the party's propaganda efforts. Though the other members of the leadership committee personally disliked Hitler, they had grown dependent on his power to organize publicity and to acquire funds for the party. He continually demanded more and more authority until finally, in July 1921, they were forced to give in and make him president with unlimited power. Anxious for more power, he tried a *putsch* against the Weimar Republic in November 1923, which failed and resulted in his arrest and imprisonment. He served only nine months of a five-year sentence, and used it to write the first volume of *Mein Kampf* ("My Struggle"). This book completely outlined Hitler's racist political ideology and "poisoned a generation and distorted the outlook of a whole people."[1]

The Nazi Party disintegrated while he was in prison, and it took him years before he was able to rebuild it. Hitler's one talent was his power of persuasion. At this point in his career, Hitler did not have any original ideas. The concepts of nationalism and anti-Marxism were commonly accepted truths of Viennese right-wing radicalism, which Hitler was exposed to in his youth. His one unique touch was to focus on the Jew. He understood that he was better able to inflame the passions of the populace when he focused on a single nemesis, and the Jewish people were a convenient target. They became for him almost mythical in their incarnation of evil. On them, Hitler projected all that he feared and hated.

After the economic slump in 1929, the masses began to flock to the Nazi Party. Hitler's inflammatory rhetoric provided answers that no one else was offering. By 1930, the Nazis were the second largest party in the country. Hitler opposed Hindenburg in the presidential election of 1932, and even though he lost, his strength forced Hindenburg to name him chancellor of Germany in January 1933. Once in power, Hitler proceeded to establish an absolute dictatorship. In just six more years, he would have all of Europe at war.

The anti-leader model is evidenced in Hitler from these roots. He was a man who took full advantage of the Leadership Conditions but had little positive Leadership Capital. Note the following:

- **Position** — Hitler was in exactly the perfect position as propaganda chief to enhance his stature in the party. Even being president of the party would not have afforded him as much stature as being the one responsible for recruitment and fundraising. Each step of his rise to power was strategic. He had just enough positional strength to pull for more authority.

- **Place** — Hitler's chief talent was his ability to arouse people, and he was in the perfect domain to do it as propaganda chief of the Nazi Party. Hitler was not an original or creative thinker. Virtually every one of his ideas came from others. What he was able to do, though, was use his oratory skills to promote these ideas to their fullest (and tragic) consequence.

- **People** — Hitler was able to outmaneuver others in leadership because they were weaker and less ambitious than he was. His propaganda machine fed the frustration of the German people from their defeat in World War I. His appeal to nationalistic pride was tailor-made for the German people.

- **Period** — Hitler's timing could not have been more perfect. Germany was devastated and looking for answers. Hitler had simple answers that filled a huge need for the German people. All of Germany's leaders had been discredited from the previous war, so there was a huge vacuum of leadership at the time of Hitler's ascent.

Hitler himself recognized these same ideal Conditions. In *Mein Kampf,* he wrote that it was an "unmerited mean trick of Fate" that he was "born in a period between two wars, at a time of quiet and order." He also attributed "Fate" to the happenstance of his birthplace, his role as a German foot soldier, and even his eventual imprisonment. Hitler arrived in a leadership position, but because his Leadership Capital was so severely limited, the end result was horrific. His vision was destructive, not constructive. His wisdom and courage was many times fatal and ineffective. His aides grew to distrust him (although they stayed loyal out of fear).

Only in the area of voice could Hitler claim true Leadership Capital, for his ability to embody a message and communicate it have had few peers. Hitler's power grew as he was more able to use this particular attribute, because voice is most needed for medium-to-large organizations. He rose quickly when he was able to utilize his chief strength in a larger domain. But because he lacked the other attributes, voice alone could not carry him.

Where Hitler failed most, though, was the competency of values. His blind rage toward the Jews, which bent him on a hellish path of vindication, can never be justified by any standard of moral decency. There is even some historical evidence that Hitler's main purpose in launching his military campaigns was to disguise his true ambition, which was the total extermination of the Jewish people.

Hitler and other demagogues serve as a sobering reminder that those who find themselves at the top are not necessarily the best or wisest—they simply were in the right place doing what they do best for the type of people who would accept them at the most advantageous time. They are not leaders. They are lucky.

The Golden Mean

No one would like to think of him or herself as an anti-leader, but the simple fact is that many leaders develop what could be called anti-leader characteristics that could cause their downfall. To understand how this can happen, we can go back to antiquity and recall the words of Aristotle from *Niccomacean Ethics (Book II)* concerning the Golden Mean. The Greeks were fascinated with the aesthetic perfection of mathematics and tried to apply it to all areas of life. Aristotle felt that just as there was an order in the natural order, man could find harmony and order with himself and others by establishing the right balance.

He established a triad of virtues where the balance lay between the defect and excess of the virtue. So, for example, a man should be liberal with his spending, but not overly frugal or overly spendthrift.

The Ideal Leadership Model uses the six core competencies of Leadership Capital as the "ideal" or correct balance, which the leader should demonstrate. Anti-leadership is the "dark side" of the Ideal Leadership Model. It is the side with an absence of light. Light is what we associate with goodness—humility, honesty, concern for one's fellow man and the environment—what could be called simple decency or good character. Darkness is a disregard for those qualities. It is the misuse of Leadership Capital that almost certainly insures failure. When leaders display these negative characteristics, their organizations are heading for trouble.

The following chart outlines the general characteristics of anti-leadership:

Anti-Leadership (Deficiency)	Ideal Leadership Competency	Anti-Leadership (Excess)
Blindness	Vision	Obsession
Amoralism/Pragmatism	Values	Intolerance/Imprudence
Foolishness/Carelessness	Wisdom	Presumption/Arrogance
Timidity	Courage	Rashness/Foolhardiness
Distrust	Trust	Groupthink
Silence	Voice	Noise

The Golden Mean in leadership is a delicate balance, which is why real leadership is so difficult and so rarely seen! Finding that right balance, and avoiding the traps on each side of the competency, requires careful examination.

Blindness (Deficiency) — VISION — Obsession (Excess)

Steven Covey took an old story and made it one of his foremost principles in *Seven Habits of Highly Effective People*. A hardworking woodsman cuts fewer and fewer trees each day until he is finally threatened with termination. He protests that he is the hardest worker in his group. He arrives first, leaves last, and rarely takes rest breaks. The foreman asks him, "When do you take time to sharpen your saw?"

Covey believes that taking the time to "sharpen the saw" is so important that he made it the seventh and encompassing principle of his personal development program. Leaders have this sense of perspective. They do not continually focus on the now (short-term gains), but they

162

consider what will be necessary to face the future and the long-term well-being of the organization.

The anti-leadership trait of blindness sees only today. In the first half of the 1990s, some successful businessmen in the Baltics took their profits and spent them on lavish vacations and expensive automobiles and clothes. They were living high. Others lived more modestly and invested their earnings in real estate, as many individuals who came into reclaimed property were anxious to offload it for immediate cash. A decade later, many of those who were living high in the now faced severe financial difficulties with little resources to meet them. Those who had invested in real estate, however, had a strong base of investment capital that they could use.

One reason why "blindness" does not seem so bad is because the long-term perspective is more difficult to see. Jesus told an interesting parable about a master who gave each of his three servants a sum of money; one received five talents, one received two talents, and the third received one talent of money. The servants with five and two talents immediately went and invested their funds, whereas the fellow with one talent went and buried his in the ground.

Now, if the three immediately sat down together for coffee at some café and discussed their fortunes, the third servant would have bragging rights! After all, his money was secure, whereas the other two had taken risks and could conceivably come back with nothing. The short-term perspective, "blindness," is difficult to argue against in the immediate circumstances. However, each of the two servants who had invested ended up doubling their money, and the other servant had only what he had started with. The master called him wicked and lazy. He was an anti-leader. He thought only of today and not of tomorrow. He had no vision.

On the other hand, taking a vision to the extreme becomes an obsession. One of the most extreme examples of this was the televangelist Oral Roberts and his City of Faith Medical and Research Center. Roberts founded a university named after himself in 1963, and by 1977 it had steadily grown in prestige and academic excellence. But in that year, Roberts literally had a vision he claimed was from God. He envisioned building on the ORU campus three skyscrapers, the tallest being Cityplex Tower standing 198 meters (648 feet) and 60 floors, the second tallest building in Oklahoma. This was to be the largest health facility of its kind in the world and would merge prayer and medicine in the healing process.

None of his board agreed with the idea, fearing the grandiose scale of the project would jeopardize the financial foundation of the entire institution. But Roberts was adamant that the project must be realized, and through tremendous fund-raising efforts, the facility was built and opened in 1981. But from the beginning, the City of Faith never realized any of its goals, and eventually closed in 1989, owing $25 million in debt.

True vision is sober of mind and stout of heart. It dwells in that balance between a focus only on the now and a fixation on the future that is neither real nor possible.

Amoralism / Pragmatism (Deficiency) – VALUES – Intolerance / Imprudence (Excess)

One of the great unsung heroes of history is William Wilberforce (1759-1833). For 40 years he led a campaign in England for the total abolition of slavery. Standing against him were powerful economic interests, which argued that slavery made good business sense.

From a pragmatic view, they were right, for abolishing slavery would have an immediate detrimental effect upon the British economy. But Wilberforce was a man of principle, and he argued vehemently that it was wrong from a moral perspective. It took decades of very hard work before he finally saw victory right before his death.

Strong moral convictions serve as an anchor against the raging sea of constant change. Unfortunately, too many of those who rise to a position of prominence see that position as an opportunity to take advantage of the four P's: pay, perks, power and prestige. They weigh alternatives based on how it will personally benefit them. They operate without any moral foundation to direct their actions and decision-making. They are pragmatists in the worst sense of the word—they use expediency and opportunity as their only guide.

When Latvia became an independent nation, a number of business-men with Latvian heritage returned to set up new enterprises. Meanwhile, my wife had helped start a charity rehabilitation clinic for children with physical disabilities. She solicited donations from these businesses appealing to their desire to help improve the welfare of the children of their country, and many responded. One Canadian-Latvian, however, actually became indignant when Debbie asked for a donation for her clinic. He told Debbie that he did not care about disabled children, or anyone else for that matter; he cared only about making as much money as he could as quickly as he could.

Every single business that has supported Debbie's rehabilitation center over the years has prospered, but this Canadian-Latvian lost his business and is now back in Canada. Giving to charity alone is not a panacea, but it is an indication of a higher value than simple profit motive. Real leaders are not shallow, but have a depth of convictions that serves them in good times and bad. The true leader does not compromise his or her convictions when they become inconvenient due to difficult circumstances.

Yet even in values there must be a balance. Though the value itself may be sound, the leader must never claim an absolute knowledge in how it is to be applied. The great philosopher and theologian Augustine of Hippo noted that one of the most valuable assets for a leader was prudence. To claim absolute certainty about anything borders on pride, and this was the root sin that caused the fall of mankind. A wise leader understands that he must always exhibit tolerance for others' viewpoints.. It never hurts to listen and learn.

Foolishness/Carelessness (Deficiency) — WISDOM — Presumption (Excess)

Anti-leaders practice poor judgment, which is exhibited in bad decisions and careless mistakes. Like anti-leader blindness, these results may not be evidenced immediately. Foolish leaders do not think through all the implications of their decisions, or consider all the necessary factors.

Hitler's decision to invade the Soviet Union certainly falls into this category. Ironically, he did not consider that another invader with a much better track record of success than he, Napoleon Bonaparte, suffered a humiliating defeat by attempting exactly the same thing. It is difficult to imagine that Hitler was not aware of that important piece of history. His pride and hubris caused him to imagine that he could do what others knew to be impossible.

Corporate executives can display the same foolishness; they simply do it with money and influence. WQED in Pittsburgh was a small public TV station in 1970 with $2 million in annual revenue. Two executives, Lloyd Kaiser and Thomas Skinner, came to Pittsburgh from a public TV station in Hershey, Pennsylvania. With their leadership, they built a station that won 28 Emmy awards, equivalent to the biggest stations in New York and Boston. They launched the incredibly successful children's program "Mister Rogers" as well as a number of specials by National Geographic, which rank among the most-watched shows ever seen on public television. Kaiser and Skinner built WQED up into a $36 million enterprise that also included a classical radio station and a popular monthly magazine. In their minds, they could do no wrong.

But by the mid-1980s, the climate had changed. State and local governments were resisting allocating the funding grants they had previously provided, corporate sponsors were focusing on other sponsorships, and the spread of cable television had seriously cut into the market share of public television. Prudent management would have noticed these changes and taken some proactive measures. Instead, WQED increased their compensation packages and continued with business as usual. After all, they thought, we are WQED. We are not like other public television stations; we are the elite, the trendsetters, the best! The end result is not hard to predict. They lost Gulf Oil, their principle sponsor, and then National Geographic, their main coproducer. Financing dried up, and WQED had to struggle to survive.

Leaders cannot afford to be foolish. William Cooper wrote, "Knowledge is proud that it knows so much; wisdom is humble that it knows no more." This humility causes the wise leader to draw on others. American president Woodrow Wilson, a brilliant man who also served as president of Princeton University, once said, "We should not only use all the brains we have, but all that we can borrow." The foolish leader presumes he knows it all. Norman Vincent Peale was right when he wrote, "The trouble with most of us is that we'd rather be ruined by praise than loved by criticism."

The foolish attempt to speak with authority from a vacuum of knowledge. Abraham Lincoln was particularly annoyed by criticism of his way of handling the war from authority figures that pretended to be wise on a minimum diet of facts and information. They would propose to offer wisdom that they did not possess. Lincoln's response (which was typical for him) was to tell a story. A traveler lost in the woods was caught in a terrific thunderstorm. His horse became mired in mud and could not continue. He stood there alone in the middle of the road while lightning streaked through the sky and the thunder roared above him. Suddenly, a loud crash seemed to shake the earth underneath him and brought the man to his knees. He was not a praying man, but because he was in the position, he offered up a short petition, "O Lord, if it is all the same to You, give me a little more light and a little less noise."

The wise leader does not offer light that he or she does not possess. Leaders hold unique knowledge; they know something that nobody else knows but needs to know. They may have what C.W. Ceran called that genius which can reduce the complicated to the simple. They may have that cleverness that looks where no one else does. As Sir Arthur Conan Doyle's character Sherlock Holmes so eloquently put it, "Once you eliminate the impossible, whatever remains, no matter how improbable, must be the truth." Wisdom is knowing what to do with that knowledge. As chessmaster Savielly Grigorievitch Tartakower put it, "Victory goes to the player who makes the next-to-last mistake."

A wise man may be ignorant, because he simply lacks knowledge. The ignorant man may obtain knowledge, and hence, no longer be ignorant.

Ignorance is not a state of being, but a circumstance. A stupid person, on the other hand, is one who is not aware of what he lacks or does not care. The worst of all is the foolish man, for he imagines himself as wise.

An old Arabian proverb states there are four sorts of men:

> *He who knows not and knows not he knows not;*
> *he is a fool—shun him.*
> *He who knows not and knows he knows not;*
> *he is simple—teach him.*
> *He who knows and knows not he knows;*
> *he is asleep—wake him.*
> *He who knows and knows he knows;*
> *he is wise—follow him.*

Wise leaders are always hungry to learn and grow. They associate with others who they know have wisdom that they can use. As Plautus has said, "No man is wise enough by himself." Leaders fall into an anti-leader syndrome when they pretend to be wise, rather than to admit their ignorance. It is foolishness; and when the stakes are high, it can be deadly.

Timidity (Deficiency) — COURAGE — Rashness / Foolhardiness (Excess)

Managers do not need to be particularly courageous, because by definition, they are maintaining the status quo. Leaders, however, do not have this luxury. They must be bold to act when action is needed. Anti-leaders are either more worried about making a mistake than taking necessary but calculated risks, or they do the opposite—rush in where angels fear to tread.

"Courage is a special kind of knowledge," wrote Israeli leader David Ben-Gurion, "the knowledge of how to fear what ought to be feared and know not to fear what ought not to be feared." Winston Churchill, among many others, felt that courage was the most valuable of leadership qualities because it guaranteed all the others. When leaders refuse to act, which is timidity, or when their main criteria for decision-making is the reduction of risk, they are practicing anti-leadership. No one can be absolutely certain that their decisions are the right ones, but leaders must act.

A ship in harbor is safe, but that is not what a ship is built for. Anti-leaders hesitate because they fear making a mistake or do not want to fail, but failure does not stop real leaders. Paul Galvin at the age of 33 had failed twice in business. He decided not to give up, however. At an auction of his failed storage-battery business, he used his last $750 to buy back the battery eliminator portion of the business. That was the beginning of a company that became known as Motorola. When Galvin retired in the 1960s he said, "Do not fear mistakes. You will know failure. Continue to reach out."

It takes courage to keep going when times are tough. Anti-leaders give up or look for an easy out. Abraham Lincoln had one of the rockiest roads to success of any great leader. In 1831, he experienced a business failure. In 1832, he was defeated for the Illinois legislature, and in 1833, he endured his *second* business failure. After finally getting elected to state office, he failed in his attempts to be elected Speaker (1838) and Elector (1840). In 1843, and again in 1848, he was defeated for U.S. Congress, and in 1855 and 1858, was defeated for the US Senate. In 1856, he was defeated for Vice President. Yet just four years after that, in 1860, he was elected President of the United States! Most men would have given up long before that time. It was that same tenacity, however, that would serve Lincoln well during those trying years that the United States was at war with itself.

As the last chapter noted, courage becomes more and more important as an organization grows in size. The most difficult decisions for the leader of a large and important organization are the ones that require courage, because the consequences are so broad. Some who were able to make the simple steps of courage in smaller domains begin to shrink when the cost becomes much, much higher.

The other side of the coin, however, consists of those who enjoy great success through daring times and believe that simply through their personal genius and force of personality, they can create the conditions under which their organization operates. Sidney Finkelstein of the Tuck School of Management at Dartmouth College calls this tendency the "illusion of personal pre-eminence."[2] This courage is reckless, and will not produce the desired result.

Distrust (Deficiency) — TRUST — Groupthink (Excess)

Anti-leaders have a very difficult time trusting people and are not trusted by others. Some historians believe that one of the principle reasons that the Union won the United States Civil War against the Confederacy was because the Confederate President, Jefferson Davis, was such a distrusting person as compared with Abraham Lincoln. Lincoln worked with individuals whom he personally did not like, but whom he knew could get the job done. Davis, on the other hand, almost admitted that if he had to choose between losing an argument and losing a friend, he would choose losing the friend.

Trust is the essential element of all interpersonal interaction, and when it is missing, the consequences are always bad and sometimes even fatal. A case in point—Wagner Dodge led a group of 15 other firefighters who had sky-jumped into a fiery gulch in Montana to put out a raging forest and grass fire on August 5, 1949. Dodge and his men raced toward the fire, seeking to keep themselves between a nearby river and the fire. But the fire was moving faster than they were, and cut off their access to the river. In the space of one hour, Dodge had his men first march toward the fire, then around it, and finally running from it.

The fire was moving faster than the men. It became apparent they could not outrun the fire, and suddenly Dodge stopped and took out his pocket lighter. He lit a small grass fire around himself and yelled to his men to stand next to him. They disregarded his plea and 13 of the men died in the fire. Dodge stood in a burned-out circle as the fire roared past him, saving his life. Had his men joined him in the circle, their lives would not have been lost.[3]

Very simply, Dodge's men did not trust him anymore. His erratic actions prior to the crisis caused them to believe that he did not know what he was doing. Leaders who give their followers reason to distrust them are displaying anti-leader tendencies.

Distrust is so serious that some researchers in organizational behavior actually consider it a form of corporate tax. I prefer to think of it like a computer virus. It slows down everything that happens in an organization. Distrust produces paranoia, and paranoia inevitably leads to draconian control measures. It prevents innovation and breeds suspicion. Any leader who recognizes distrust among his or her followers should immediately seek to root it out. It is organizational poison.

The other extreme is just as deadly—the virus known as Groupthink. Irving Janis coined this phrase, which has earned a place as a classic in social psychology.[4] Janis cites the Bay of Pigs fiasco under President Kennedy's administration as the archetype of Groupthink due to the blind trust exhibited. It happens when people get together in insular groups to make decisions, often blinded by the trust they have in their leader. The individuals in the organization trust only themselves and close themselves off to anyone outside their group. It has become described as similar to a riot mentality—the group becomes a mind of its own.

In general, however, the Aristotelian mean should favor more trust rather than less. Too much trust is a caution to watch for, but continually building trust is a worthwhile endeavor for all leaders.

Silence (Deficiency) — VOICE — Noise (Excess)

The Bible quotes, *"For if the trumpet give*[s] *an uncertain sound, who shall prepare himself* [for] *the battle?"* (1 Cor. 14:8 KJV). Voice is the clarity of message that leaders give to their followers. It is the articulation of their vision and values in concrete, objective, inspiring, and understandable language, which is consistent with their practice. When the leader's voice is clear, people take action.

Anti-leaders are either silent, making their followers guess their intentions, or they make "sounds"—they are not a clear voice. This is simply noise. I once worked as a division director in the Philadelphia area for a large corporation that had its head office in New York City. The first time the big boss paid us a visit, he told me that he did not like my office and that I should change it. I was young and too intimidated to ask what I was thinking, *Change it to what?* Did he mean it was too cluttered? Did he object to the color of paint on the walls? Did he want me to move my desk? And further, I wondered, *Why was my office décor an area of interest to him?* I was the one who had to work in my office; he had his own in New York City.

After giving it some thought, I decided to disregard the remark. It did not make sense, and I reasoned that I had more important matters to worry about because I had taken over an operation that was doing very, very poorly. About six months later, the boss from New York returned, and we reviewed our sales numbers that had considerably improved since his last visit. As he was getting ready to leave, he looked at me and remarked, "I am glad you got your office in order."

It suddenly struck me what the man had meant before. When he was talking about the "office," he was referring to operational systems. By "changing" he meant, "get your numbers up." He was using in-house jargon that I was totally unfamiliar with.

He thought he had clearly directed me (judging by the results), but in reality, I paid no attention to his words at all. They were just noise.

J. Edgar Hoover, former head of the FBI, once wrote on a document "watch the borders" because the margins of the pages were too narrow. His agents immediately began patrolling the Mexican and Canadian borders of the United States! Though it seems humorous to us, think of the countless man-hours and money wasted every day because leaders do not communicate correctly and effectively.

Parents learn this early on in their child rearing. I found that when I told my children it was time for them to go to bed, they would disregard me. They knew that I would give them at least two warnings, then my voice would rise, then I would threaten—and it was then that they had better obey! So every night we went through the same ritual because they had learned my "voice" and what it really meant.

One of the common complaints about leadership training is that when the business leaders try to communicate to their staff their newfound discoveries, their staffs are less than impressed. Why? Because they sense it is someone else's voice they are hearing, and not their boss. It is only when subordinates see a change in their superior's behavior, that the boss is really "walking the walk and not just talking the talk," that they will begin to sit up and take notice.

When leaders are merely ordering and commanding, they are simply making noise. Noise is loud and cannot be disregarded. We pay attention to noise because it is difficult not to. But noise is unpleasant.

Noise is hard to listen to for a very long period of time. Noise eventually deafens the listeners.

Yet silence is just as bad. John H. Gutfreund is one example. Gutfreund was chairman and chief executive officer of Salomon Brothers, one of Wall Street's richest companies. A brilliant bond trader and power broker, he had been featured on the cover of *Business Week* as the "King of Wall Street."[5] Yet within just six months in 1991, he virtually bankrupted his company. He made a series of bad decisions that went back to not reporting a fraud made in a U.S. Treasury bond purchase by his top trader.

The chairman of the U.S. Securities and Exchange Commission, Richard Breeden, would later describe this inaction as a "long and thunderous silence." John Gutfreund sat on a time bomb and let it go off.[6] How did this happen? Here was a man who was obviously quite successful, but suddenly when faced with a major leadership decision, did not seem adequate to the task. His GOLI turned into a FOLI through his silence.

Of all the competencies, having the right voice is perhaps the most difficult of all, because communication depends greatly on the perception of the individual who is receiving the message. This is why a voice must be consistent over a long period of time. Maintaining a constant voice also can disarm critics when a contrary message might be suggested.

Several times in my life individuals who are absolutely convinced they are right have falsely accused me, in some cases rather vehemently. My defense in every case was my voice.

When a professor visiting Latvia objected to my dismissal of several older Russian women from a lecture that was meant for Latvian young people, he reported back in the United States that Larry Stout was obviously prejudiced against Russians. My associates in Latvia immediately rose to my defense and asked how this could be true when Larry had so many Russian friends, attended and taught at Russian church for years, and even adopted a Russian daughter! In this case, my actions spoke louder than the words of my accuser.

Anti-Leader Prevention

Anti-leadership is the dark side of the pyramid. It happens when leaders have not developed or used their true Leadership Capital. There are several reasons why this happens. First, leaders get comfortable in their present condition. They enjoy the fruits of success as they are experiencing them, and see no reason to develop and grow. Ironically, they may have used Leadership Capital in the past, but then got lazy and fell into an anti-leadership mode. In the short run, anti-leadership can make an individual look and feel very good.

King David of the Bible went through this experience. He had been a king for some time and had fought many battles through the years. Though his kingdom was enjoying relative tranquility, there were still enemy armies lurking about that needed to be vanquished. However, King David decided he did not need to lead his troops into the battlefield as he had in the past. He was enjoying being king, and thought that he deserved to take it easy for a while. It was during this respite that he noticed a beautiful woman taking a bath. Flames of passion were aroused, and as king, he decided he had the right to satisfy his desires.

Unfortunately, the woman, Bathsheba, became pregnant. Even more unfortunate was that she was married to a soldier who was away fighting (as David should have been). David quickly arranged for the husband to have a furlough back home, hoping that he would have relations with his wife and get David off the hook. But the soldier was so dedicated that he chose not to sleep with his wife while his comrades-in-arms were suffering in the field.

David's infidelity took a criminal turn, when he decided to have this brave soldier put on the front lines so he would be killed. The plan worked, and David took the new widow as his bride. This action resulted in years of hardship and difficulty for David, and even the death of the child who was birthed as a result of the initial sexual encounter. David was a great man and a great king—but in this instance, he acted like an anti-leader. He used his power for personal advantage and even committed a crime to hide it.

Another reason anti-leadership tendencies become easier is because developing true Leadership Capital takes time and effort. Anti-leadership usually comes more naturally. I have taught literally thousands of business people and government officials in Latvia and Russia, and a common complaint voiced to me about my theories are that they require so much work to implement. I have to agree with them. Developing wisdom is not something that is done in a weekend. Acquiring a leader's vision takes tremendous effort to overcome preconceived ideas and prejudices. (With our last leadership essential, we will discuss in detail this important facet of continually developing leadership competencies.)

Still another reason for the prevalence of anti-leadership characteristics in so many of today's leaders is due to the "tyranny of the urgent." Warren Bennis identifies an "unconscious conspiracy" that forces the person at the top of an organization to spend an inordinate amount of time on routine tasks. These are the fires that every business, company, organization, or group experiences; and it is the leader's job to put them out.

However noble and fulfilling fire fighting might be, it is essentially a *preventative* measure. It seeks to limit damage. Real leadership is a *progressive* measure; it is building for the future.

Richard Johnson was headmaster of Penn Christian Academy in Norristown, Pennsylvania, where I also served as school board president during the decade of the 1980s. Richard was unquestionably one of the hardest working individuals I have ever known, and fought the "unconscious conspiracy" every single day. I can still picture us walking down a hallway to his office and seeing him pick up a gum wrapper, pat a student on the head, speak briefly with a teacher, encourage a parent volunteer—and simultaneously continue a running conversation with me!

At the same time, Richard never ceased to develop his Leadership Capital. He was always learning, always planning, always seeking ways to make the school better in the future than it had been before. As busy as Richard was with his day-to-day operations, he took time daily to increase his personal Leadership Capital through maintaining his vision, acquiring wisdom, exhibiting courage, building trust with his staff, making sure his message was clear, and standing uncompromisingly on a solid base of values. Richard was an unfortunate victim of cancer in 1996, but he left an indelible mark on everyone who knew him.

Anti-leadership is something like the oxidation of metal, which causes rust. Rust is caused by a piece of metal not being properly coated or well maintained. If a spot of rust is caught in time, it can be quickly and easily dealt with and not cause any permanent damage. But if the rust is left to grow, it will result in deterioration of the metal that cannot be repaired, only replaced.

Leadership Capital requires work, just as keeping an automobile clean and shiny requires serious effort. If leaders, for whatever reason, succumb to anti-leadership characteristics, they will head down a road that will not produce success for their organizations. If they catch themselves in time, they can turn around and work toward positive growth and perhaps even be a better leader in the long run. But if they stay on the dark side of the pyramid, the organization will find itself with no other choice than eliminating the anti-leader for its own survival.

In the end, there is no real alternative. Developing the six competencies of Leadership Capital is the only productive choice leaders can make if they truly care about building their organization toward a goal of continual success.

The mediocre leader tells, the good leader explains, the superior leader demonstrates, and the great leader inspires.

Buchholz and Roth

---------------- Endnotes ----------------

1. U.S. Government Document. *Nazi Aggression and Conspiracy –* Volume 1, Chapter 9, Section 6; http://fundamentalbass. home.mindspring.com/x5866.html

2. "Finkelstein, Sidney. Seven Habits of Spectacularly Unsuccessful People" *Business Strategy Review*, Vol. 14, Issue 4 (Winter 2003).

3. Maclean, Norman. *Young Men and Fire* (University of Chicago, Chicago, IL, 1993).

4. Janis, Irving. *Groupthink: Psychological Studies of Policy Decisions and Fiascos* (Houghton Mifflin, Boston, MA, 1982).

5. Bianco, Anthony. "The King of Wall Street," *Business Week* (December 9, 1985).

6. Grant, Linda. "Taming the Bond Buccaneers at Solomon Brothers," *Los Angeles Times Magazine* (February 16, 1992).

Key Ideas

1. Failure in leadership is a result of changing Conditions or mis-applied Capital.

2. For each of the Leadership Capital competencies, there are deficiencies and extremes, which when exhibited will result in "anti-leadership."

3. The best preventative to anti-leadership is continually developing good Leadership Capital.

Questions for Active Leaders

1. What do you believe was the worst mistake you have made as a manager or leader? What characteristic of anti-leadership would you attribute this to? Have you taken steps to prevent a similar event in the future?

2. How "balanced" do you believe you are in the Leadership Capital areas? Where do you think you might need some realignment?

Questions for FLOWters (Future Leaders of the World)

1. Even great leaders can lean from time to time towards anti-leadership tendencies. What do you attribute this to? How could it be prevented?

2. Choose any leader who has been in the news lately. Do you recognize any anti-leadership characteristics in them?

CHAPTER NINE

The Seventh Essential—
The Importance of Continuation

Super Seven

Through the course of these seven essentials, we have discussed several times the dynamic between management and leadership. Management is maintaining status quo—keeping the systems running, making sure things are getting done as they should. Leadership is breaking out into new directions, charting new paths, shaking up the status quo to keep up with the changes in the world at large.

Leadership is often called an art as much as a science. This is because it is necessary to know how to balance the need for leadership with the essential day-to-day management operations without which the organization would fail to function properly. Echoing the words President Bush used to describe the transformation of the United States Armed Forces, how do you tune an engine that is racing down the road at 80 miles an hour?

Somehow leadership must find a way to overhaul the engine without shutting it down. I witnessed this firsthand living in Latvia since 1991. The independent Republic of Latvia instantly emerged after the collapse of the Soviet Union. Unfortunately, the newly independent country did not have the luxury of stopping the world until it was able to get its house in order. It carried some vestiges of the Soviet system as it transitioned to a democratic and free market society. However, it has been slowly chipping away at these anachronistic practices over the years. Rome was not built in a day, and neither is a country.

But all this leadership initiative is drawn from the Leadership Capital that a leader has *already* developed. The challenges of the future will require still more Capital, and this must be acquired. A wealthy man once told me, "Larry, it is not hard to make a lot of money. The trick is to keep it." Though he was talking about taxes and investments, I believe the same truth can be applied to Leadership Capital. The seventh leadership essential concept is: ***Leadership Capital is an expendable resource***.

Oil companies make their money selling oil and gas, of course, but these are expendable resources. The companies must constantly search for new reserves to replace the sources that run out.

A company's stock price is not just related to the price of oil, but also directly related to those reserves. In 2005, the Royal Dutch/Shell Group of Companies was forced to pay $90 million to settle a lawsuit to its investors because the company had overestimated its oil and gas reserves by as much as 25 percent. Leaders should take note. Though they may be riding high today, their future success is directly related to the Leadership Capital they are developing for that future.

Just like the oil company, discovering these leadership reserves for later use involves hard work! It will not just happen on its own. The best way to approach this is through a conscious design—a personal lifetime leadership plan.

Warren Bennis wrote an intriguing article[1] outlining the stages of a leader's life based on William Shakespeare's "seven ages of man" passage in the play, *As You Like It*. Before examining these specific stages of a leader, it is worth first considering the significance of the number *seven*. We have been referring to the seven leadership essentials, and again we find ourselves with a list of seven. What is it about this number?

Psychological research in the 20th century has shown a remarkable phenomenon—the reoccurrence of the number *seven* as a number of completion. George Miller made a landmark study in 1956 on the brain's ability to process information. He claimed that he was being "persecuted by an integer." It was the number *seven*. His research led him to conclude that the mind can channel only seven inputs or "bits" of information at one time. (To get an idea of what Miller is talking about, glance quickly at a table with many objects on it and then try to recall what was on the table. You will probably not remember many more than seven individual items). Further, Miller concluded that the short-term memory holds this information in approximately seven units or "chunks" (which might explain why telephone numbers were initially combined in groups of seven, Snow White met seven dwarfs, and the medieval church listed seven deadly sins, etc.) Miller was so fascinated by this that he called the number *seven* "magical."[2]

Howard Gardner was heading up Project Zero at Harvard University that was started without any presuppositions about thinking processes (hence the name of the project, starting from zero), and their research led them to conclude that there are seven "intelligences": verbal, math, kinetic, music, spatial, interpersonal, and intrapersonal.[3]

Nature itself seems to verify that seven represents the limits of capacity. There are seven colors in the spectrum, seven notes in the music scale, seven continents on the earth, and sailors once spoke of sailing the seven seas. The seven-day week is an anthropological phenomenon that cannot be explained by astronomical observation as the day, month, and year. The origin of week dates back to antiquity, most likely from the biblical allusion of God's creation of the earth in six days and resting on the seventh.

Why is this attention to the number *seven* so important? There is something about the number *seven* that speaks of completion.

It is not a random number. If we are going to design a complete lifetime leadership program, it should be in seven phases. Warren Bennis described these phases as stages in the life of the leader: infant, schoolboy, lover, soldier, general, statesman, and sage. We will take these concepts and note how each one can be designed to be a self-renewing process in Leadership Capital.

Infant Stage: Acquire Values

There is a Latin expression, *finis origine pendet,* which means "the end depends upon the beginning." A good start will have much to do with later success. Bennis emphasizes the importance of quickly finding a mentor in the "infant" stage of leadership development to help shape the direction the leader will take.

In developed Western nations, this is good advice. A good mentor is an invaluable resource. I was blessed with two extremely wonderful men who have been mentioned previously, Richard Johnson in education, and Tom Jamison in management, who left an indelible mark upon me though both men departed this earth much too soon.

But in many parts of the world, especially those in developing nations, there are not many mentors available, and those who are around might not be ones who should be emulated! What to do when the options are limited? In these cases, experience has shown us that there are other routes that the new leader can follow.

The best alternative to a mentor is to find another person in the same boat. But instead of sharing ignorance, seek together to find the answers. The synergy of another person can make a tremendous difference. The most difficult course at Stockholm School of Economics in Riga is a course in Financial Economics. Every year, only about ten percent of the students pass the mid-term exam the first time they take it. But year after year, *it is the students who study with a partner who make up that ten percent.*

What can the leader and his or her partner do? For one thing, they can read good literature and discuss it. This does not mean reading only articles and books specifically about leadership, but using fiction and nonfictional biographies to learn about application of leadership. Every culture is rich in examples of leaders and their stories.

For example, I had many enriching discussions with a couple of friends in my university days as we read about Prince Hal in William Shakespeare's plays, *Henry IV, Part 1 and Henry IV, Part 2.* Shakespeare's tragedies such as *Hamlet, King Lear,* and *Macbeth* are much more well-known, but we identified with bad boy Hal. He seemed to be running away from responsibility, but it kept finding him. We could see growth and development that took place in his life despite his hedonism, and when Hal assumed the mantle of leadership in Henry V, it was obvious he was a mature man. We used this example to analyze our own development and speculate about our own mistakes that could be learning experiences to build wisdom in us.

If literature does not work, there are popular films. I watched *Batman Begins* with my youngest son Aaron, and afterward we discussed the film for over two hours. It had a goldmine of examples about leadership development, but they needed to be dug out.

Before an individual can lead, he must have some sense of why he wants to lead, how he wants to lead, who he looks up to and why. This is the principle key to beginning a life of leadership—having some sense of values from which to choose what is important, what is worth devoting energy toward, and what is to be avoided at all costs.

Many young people have benefited from actively associating with a church or synagogue. Fifty years ago in the city of Pittsburgh, Pennsylvania, an Episcopal minister named Sam Shoemaker was asked to speak to a group of young businessmen at a luncheon. In that talk, he challenged them to an experiment—for the next 30 days they were to run their businesses like they thought Jesus would run them. The men came back the next month with incredible stories, and an organization was birthed known as the Pittsburgh Experiment that still exists to this day.

Shoemaker knew that people in the work-world face difficult questions and need a moral framework to answer them. In my own training courses, I have developed my own little 30-day experiment using the Book of Proverbs in the Bible. It has 31 short chapters that can be easily read daily over a month's time. Keeping a notebook and marking particularly thought-stimulating passages and discussing these with a friend or colleague can be extremely beneficial in developing a better moral foundation.

At the Infant Stage of Leadership, focus on acquiring **values**, and for this it is necessary to get help! Find a mentor and if none is available, find a colleague so "iron can sharpen iron." Seek to develop a core base of values and then test that value set against the circumstances viewed in the surrounding world.

> VALUES
>
> The role of science, its civic role, is growing and becoming the decisive factor in society. But it is a contradictory role, in the same way that society is contradictory. The lesson of Einstein is that in all these contradictions one ought to be firmly guided by moral criteria. One may err from time to time, but one has to be ready to submit one's actions to these universal moral criteria.
>
> *Andrei Sakharov*
>
> You have to have your heart in the business and the business in your heart.
>
> *Thomas J. Watson, Sr.*, Founder and first President of IBM
> (His favorite saying)

Schoolchild Stage: Build Trust

There is an old adage about visitors who come to Latvia. After one day, they think they know everything about the country; after a week, they are made aware that there are a few things they do not understand; and after a month, they realize that they do not understand anything about the country! Unfortunately, leaders forget this Principle of Declining Assurance with Greater Awareness and attempt to come into a new organization and make immediate changes before knowing much of anything about the culture or people who work there.

It is difficult for a new leader to practice restraint, especially when he is expected to become a messiah for the organization, but the best practice is to work on winning trust. As we have mentioned several times already, trust is the essential ingredient in all interpersonal interaction. Dale

Carnegie notes that two months spent becoming genuinely interested in other people will be more effective than spending two years trying to get them interested in you.

This is a mutual learning time, for as Warren Bennis notes, leadership without mutual trust is a contradiction in terms. I acquired a summer job during my university years working at a bakery. I labored during the "graveyard" shift, from 11 in the evening till 7 in the morning. It was tiring work, and also frustrating because when things broke down, we often had to fend for ourselves to fix them. After one particularly trying work shift, I was cleaning up, and a nicely dressed gentleman who I had never seen before came up and asked me how things were going. I told him frankly that they were not going very well, but that was to be expected because no one cared about third-shift workers.

He asked about my particular concerns and listened patiently as I told him my frustrations. He thanked me and went on his way, and I forgot all about it till the next day when I went into work and found a note in my locker. It was from the president of the company, thanking me for the input! The company owned bakeries all over the country, yet this man had taken the time to come in to one of the factories before dawn, just to hear from one of the summer help. Word traveled throughout the whole plant, and our respect for management went sky-high, especially when we saw changes in the very areas of our concern.

Building trust should never stop, but in the beginning of a leader's tenure, it is critical. Workers need to see the vision and values of the leader. They need to know the stature of the man or woman who is leading them. When I became a school board president, I spent time meeting with teachers, parents, administration, and even students to hear their opinion on the school's operations. I told them I would not be able to make everyone happy at all times, but they could be sure that every decision I made was with the school's best interests in mind. Because they knew I took the time to listen, they believed and trusted me. When times got tough, we needed that trust, and it was there.

At the Schoolchild Stage of Leadership, focus on winning **trust**, and for this it is necessary to spend time and listen to people. Allocate time in the schedule to simply know what others are thinking and feeling.

Active listening is a skill even more difficult to master than speaking—but a true leader must learn it.

TRUST

The accumulation of trust is a measure of the legitimacy of leadership.

Warren Bennis

Growth is directly proportionate to promises made; profit is inversely proportionate to promises kept.

John Peers

The Lover Stage: Focus on Vision

The third stage in a leader's life is not unlike one's first love. The world suddenly becomes a different place when love is in the air. The woman I eventually married was a sister of one of my best male friends. I had known Debbie for years, but never really took particular notice of her. One day I was visiting my friend when I saw her sitting on the couch knitting, and I thought to myself how attractive she looked. I finally got the nerve to ask her out, and we never looked back. After 32 years of marriage, I realize I made a good choice.

Just as a lover focuses on his or her love, so a leader, as he is growing in his position, needs to find exactly what needs his attention. By this stage of development, the leader is familiar with the people surrounding him, the operations of the organization, and the other essential functions. But if he hopes to initiate change, he has to know where to begin.

In the early 1990s, my wife and I met with the Health Minister for Latvia. He knew of our efforts in assisting with the medical needs of children, and we told him that we would like to know what *his* priorities were for the country and how we might assist in them. He told us that any help we could bring would be appreciated. I told him that was not my question—I specifically wanted to know what his priorities were so we could best assist the country in its medical development. I even offered to help him set up a task force to develop such a plan if it did not exist. But he simply repeated that because the country needed help in every way, it did not matter in what way we helped.

I left the meeting quite frustrated. I told my wife, "He is going to regret what he is saying now. He will get all kinds of help, and won't know what to do with it." Sure enough, donations arrived in a helter-skelter fashion.

They received new medical equipment but without trained specialists who knew how to use it, old medical equipment that simply was redundant and not needed, and other equipment that was needed but had arrived with major adjustments still needed because the specifications given were wrong. The same problem came in pharmaceutical donations and even with physicians and other medical specialists willing to come and donate their services.

Much of the aid that was donated during the early 1990s was not used effectively, if at all. All the good will of those who wished to help these emerging countries could have been effectively channeled if someone at the top would have taken the time to map out a better strategy. It was true that the medical community needed lots of help, but that did not mean to throw the door open and let anyone and everyone come in.

Having a clear vision also frees up a leader to focus on what he must do instead of being distracted by the "tyranny of the urgent." One valuable lesson for leaders at this stage is to learn to focus on *only* what they need to handle to keep the organization strategically on track with the vision. A good question a leader should ask himself or herself about any activity is, "Can someone else do this besides me?" The leader should spend the majority of his time on tasks that he or she and only he or she can do. Ironically, a leader learns that it is often possible to accomplish more by doing less.

Vitali is a brilliant young entrepreneur who developed a small but growing business, but realized that his success was dependent upon hiring and training clever workers whom he could trust. He would work major clients, and it might take as much as six months to land an important one. He could not afford to divert his attention toward the mundane when he was focusing all his attention toward growing the marketing base. As he saw it, every minute he had to help on routine matters took away from building for the future.

Focus also means to pay attention to words. The Greek historian Thucydides noted many years ago, "If wisdom's ways you'd wisely seek, five things observe with care; of whom you speak, to whom you speak, and how, and when, and where. So remarkably perverse is the nature of man that he despises those that court him and admires whoever will not bend before him."

Many leaders get into trouble because they make a statement or promises that they later regret. A very good friend was visiting me in Latvia, and in the space of 24 hours made three commitments that he thought were small, but that I knew were going to result in great difficulty for him to keep. I finally took him aside and said, "Don, you are a good friend and I love you like a brother, but if you make one more obligation, I am going to break both your arms and legs and put you on a plane in a body cast!" He got the point and later realized what I was talking about. What he thought would take a couple of phone calls ended up resulting in over a year's worth of work.

At the Lover Stage of Leadership, focus on loving the organization's **vision**; and for this, it is necessary to become free from all distractions. Good leaders never stop developing their focus. They fine-tune their focus so they are maximizing their energies exactly toward what will produce the most benefit.

VISION

The greater danger for most of us is not that our aim is too high and we miss it, but that it is too low and we reach it.

Michelangelo

We choose to go to the moon in this decade and do the other things, not because they are easy, but because they are hard, because that goal will serve to organize and measure the best of our energies and skills, because that challenge is one that we are willing to accept, one we are unwilling to postpone, and one we intend to win.

John F. Kennedy

The Soldier Stage: Stay Ready With Wisdom

Those who have only been exposed to military people through films or television often have a distorted view about men and women in uniform. The vast majority do not lust for war. They are not anxious to risk their lives. Quite the contrary, they hope that their military skills will not be needed, because they know what awful costs wars bring. But one thing they do hold is that they want to act honorably. If their country calls on their service, they are ready.

That state of readiness comes from vigilance, commitment, and a certain amount of humility. Why humility? Because those who think they already know everything are not willing to learn more. Only those who know that they are incomplete seek for more wisdom. Soldiers must always be ready for whatever is asked of them.

I have a saying that "a person does not grow old, but when they stop growing, they become old." The leader who has been in place for some time begins to believe he can handle any challenge. In a Darwinian sense, it is true, because if he is still in charge, it means he has been able to survive despite the tests to his leadership. But the good leader keeps a healthy attitude of humility.

It is easy to give into a rhythm where little mental energy needs to be expended because the patterns are so well established. This was the problem with the leadership of Pan Am Airlines. For decades they dominated commercial air travel yet eventually went bankrupt. Pan Am pioneered commercial aviation in 1927. They were the first to introduce air travel across the Pacific by 1935 and the first to start commercial jet travel in 1958. In addition, they created customer innovations, like economy-class flying in the 1950s and computerized booking in the 1960s. They were flying high (a little pun intended here).

But the world was changing, and Pan Am was not changing with it. They missed the early signs that began in the 1960s and continued for the next two decades—rising fuel prices, mounting financial losses, stronger competition, and decreased government support after deregulation. Instead of exerting the leadership they had displayed in the past, they continued to act as they had when they were controlling the market.

At the Soldier Stage of Leadership, stay sharp through training and continually learning—in short, building **wisdom**. Leaders who are succeeding in growing enterprises must recognize that their greatest danger is success! They must stay sharp by staying humble. Keep listening, keep learning, keep ready.

WISDOM

It is the capacity to develop and improve their skills that distinguishes leaders from followers.

Warren Bennis and Burt Nanus

The foolish attempt to speak with authority from a vacuum of knowledge.

Abraham Lincoln

The General Stage: Exercise Courage

Courage and leadership go together like a bride and groom at a wedding—they both need each other to make it happen. Simply to act courageous for no purpose is fruitless; while leadership that is timid and fearful will never inspire others to follow. This is why traditionally even a bad leader who is not afraid to make a decision is better than one who seems to be unable to choose between unpopular options.

When an organization has grown to a size and importance where leading it has consequences for a sizeable number of people, every decision the leader makes requires courage.

General George Patton was considered one of the most courageous generals in American history. His style was criticized by many because during battles he seemed to make snap decisions. Patton took great exception to this remark. He responded, "I've been studying the subject of war for forty-odd years. When a surgeon decides in the course of an operation to change its objective, to splice that artery or cut deeper and remove another organ which he finds infected, he is not making a snap decision but one based on knowledge, experience, and training. So am I."[4]

Patton certainly made his fair share of mistakes in judgment, but he was right enough that he became one of the most successful generals during World War II. Contrast his actions with a man who had all the opportunity to be a great leader, but instead is remembered for his weakness and failures due to indecisions—George Brinton McClellan (1826-1885) who commanded the Union army for President Abraham Lincoln at the start of the American Civil War.

An able organizer, McClellan thoroughly reorganized and drilled the Army of the Potomac and instilled in its recruits a new confidence in their military potential after their bitter first defeat with the Confederate forces. In return they developed deep feelings of loyalty and affection toward him. But McClellan was more afraid of losing a battle than winning one. Cautious by nature and believing his forces to be heavily outnumbered, when the reverse was actually true, he constantly manufactured reasons for his seemingly endless string of delays. In his battle engagements, he had the uncanny ability to snatch defeat out of the jaws of victory. Lincoln tolerated the "Little Napoleon" for as long as he could, but finally, McClellan was relieved of command.

Senior leaders know that the tough decisions are never easy, but they must be made, and the best must be made of the consequences. Donald Sull notes that good firms go bad when they suffer from "active inertia." They see market changes coming, but respond by doing more of what they had done in the past.[5] The research of another business professor, Sydney Finkelstein of the Dartmouth's Tuck School of Business, also concludes the same thing. One of the leading causes of business failures was the lack of will to change course.[6]

At the General Stage of Leadership, be willing to make the tough decisions through *courage*. Leaders who want to continue to develop their Leadership Capital must resist the desire to rest on their laurels. The greatest temptation for a man at the top is to neglect the wisdom, experience, and courage it took to get there. Even the greatest king in Israel's history, King David, got soft when things became comfortable.

Instead of exercising courage in fighting battles, he spent his time watching his neighbor's wife bathe. Leaders who expect to keep leading must not forget to get out in front of the troops.

COURAGE

Far better it is to dare mighty things, to win glorious triumphs, even though checkered by failure, than to take rank with those poor spirits who neither enjoy much nor suffer much, because they live in the gray twilight that knows neither victory nor defeat.

Theodore Roosevelt

To avoid criticism—do nothing, say nothing, be nothing.

Elbert Hubbard

The Statesman Stage: Use Voice

It takes decades for a leader to truly embody a message. Mother Theresa, Martin Luther King, Jr., Nelson Mandela—to name a few—speak a message with their lifestyle that is even louder than the words they uttered.

An example of this in the business world is Warren Buffett. The Oracle of Omaha, the world's greatest stock market investor, is considered by many one of the wisest (and wealthiest) men alive. His annual salary as Berkshire Hathaway's chairman and CEO is $100,000, but his net worth as of 2005 was over $44 billion dollars.

At the age of 75, he still eats burgers or steaks for lunch and dinner, always washing down his meals with Coca-Cola—a company in which he has invested since 1988. His sole extravagance seems to be a fondness for luxury air travel. In typically self-deprecating style, the frugal Buffett calls his Gulfstream IV-SP jet "The Indefensible."

If Buffett's lifestyle seems out of step, so is his investment strategy. At a time when day traders bid up stocks based on nothing but rumor and momentum, when bond investors place pricey and complex bets on such arcane financial instruments as interest-rate futures, it's hard not to think of Buffett as a kind of museum piece. His approach is simple, even quaint. Ignoring both macroeconomic trends and Wall Street fashions, he looks for undervalued companies with low overhead costs, high growth potential, strong market share, and low price-to-earning ratios, and then waits for the rest of the world to catch up.

As often as not, Buffett's business instincts become conventional wisdom. In 1988, when Buffett started buying the global soft-drink giant Coca-Cola, it was a Wall Street wallflower, trading at $10.96. But Buffett saw two things that were not reflected in the balance sheet: the world's strongest brand name and untapped sales potential overseas. As Coca-Cola's earnings grew, so did investor interest. In less than five years, the stock soared to $74.50. Buffett's current stake is valued at some $13 billion.

Warren Buffett's secret is staying within what he calls his "circle of competency." He invests only in companies that he understands. During the hot Dot Com days of the 1990s, investors in Berkshire Hathaway's stock clamored for Buffett to jump on the bandwagon, but he resisted, because he did not understand tech stocks. Many thought of it as being old-fashioned, but it was actually practicing wisdom. When the Dot Com bubble burst, his wisdom was vindicated.

The entire man's life and lifestyle speaks of prudence in judgment. When he writes his annual stockholders letter (which is almost always a classic of brevity and sound judgment), it has a "Buffett" ring to it. He is consistent, and as a result, his voice has power.

At the Statesman Stage of Leadership—continue to hold a consistent **voice**. A leader who is dependable, steady, and embodying a message within a lifestyle of action is one who everyone wants to follow.

Voice

The best way to send an idea is to wrap it up in a person.

Robert Oppenheimer

That man can compress the most words into the smallest idea of anyone I know.

Abraham Lincoln

The Sage Stage: Mentor Others

Nothing is more beautiful than watching great athletes at the height of their powers, nor as pathetic as watching them hang on far too long after those powers have waned. One leader who did not hang on too long was Konosuke Matsushita, founder of Panasonic. He founded his company in 1917, and through the decades pioneered innovations in a number of electronic and consumer goods such as televisions, refrigerators, washing machines, and high performance audio products.

But what made Matsushita so innovative was his mission to help society by making high-quality, low-priced conveniences while providing his employees with good working conditions, earning him the sobriquet, "the god of business management." His managerial methods included customer service (long before anyone in the West thought about it), efficient production and quality products, and what has been called "pure entrepreneurialism."

Matsushita was a legend in the industry featured on the covers of *Time* and *Life* in 1962. Yet at the height of his fame and success, he shocked the world by stepping down. At the annual management policy meeting in 1961, Matsushita delivered a rousing speech, proclaiming that the company had achieved the aims of its five-year plan and was entering a new phase of growth. After completing his address, he surprised the assembled by announcing his resignation, saying, "I have just celebrated my 65th birthday. I have been thinking that I should step down at an appropriate moment, and that time has now arrived. I will continue to support the company from behind the scenes as chairman."

A true leader knows how to pass on the reins at the right time. No one can stay at the top forever, and the truly wise know when to say "when." And in stepping aside, the experienced leader is now free to impart the experience of his Leadership Capital into a new generation.

At the Sage Stage of Leadership—step aside to let others rise up, but be there to lend the hand others need as they grow into their position. Good leaders leave a legacy, not in marble statues, but in the flesh and blood of others who share their Leadership Capital.

Final Thoughts

Some physiologists claim that with body cells continually dying and being created, the entire human body is "re-created" every seven years. But because this process is happening on a continuous basis, we do not wake up every seven years feeling like a different person. Applying this same principle to leadership, we can think of the Seven Ages of the Leader not only as a sequential process, but also a simultaneous one. At every moment in life, we are living each of the seven stages, continually gaining Leadership Capital and as Conditions dictate, we apply the acquired Capital.

There are no shortcuts to leadership development. John F. Kennedy stated that leadership and learning are inseparable from one another. Nelson Mandela, one of the truly great leadership examples of the 20th century, noted, "Education is the great engine of personal development. It is through education that the daughter of a peasant can become a doctor, that the son of a mineworker can become the head of the mine, that a child of farmworkers can become the president of a great nation. It is what we make out of what we have, not what we are given, that separates one person from another."[7]

Larry's Leadership Credo

"I believe in the possibilities of unlimited vision, unshakeable values, unassailable wisdom, unbelievable courage, undying trust, and unwavering voice. I will aspire to these through growing wise and exerting courage, pursuing an inspiring vision which is based on solid values, exemplifying and communicating it all to those who trust me enough to follow my path."

Endnotes

1. Bennis, Warren. "The Seven Ages of the Leader" *Harvard Business Review*, (January 2004), 46-53.

2. Miller, George. "The magical number seven, plus or minus two: Some limits on our capacity for processing information." *The Psychological Review*, Vol 63 (1956), 81-97.

3. Gardner, Howard. *Frames of Mind: The Theory of Multiple Intelligence* (Basic Books, New York, NY, 1984). Gardner has since added an eighth intelligence, naturalist intelligence, and admits that there may be others, although his original research was very convincing for the original seven.

4. Puryear, Edgbar F. *Nineteen Stars: A Study in Military Character and Leadership* (Green Publishers, Orange, VA, 1971).

5. Sull, Donald. *Revival of the Fittest: Why Good Companies Go Bad and How Great Managers Remake Them* (Harvard Business School Press, Cambridge, MA, 2003).

6. Finkelstein, Sydney. *Why Smart Executives Fail: What You Can Learn From Their Mistakes* (Portfolio, New York, NY, 2003).

7. Mandela, Nelson. *Long Walk to Freedom* (Little, Brown and Co., London, UK).

Key Ideas

1. Leadership Capital is an expendable resource.

2. Developing Leadership Capital is a lifetime process.

3. Development in leadership can be paralleled to the "seven stages of man."

Questions for Active Leaders

1. What stage do you see yourself at the present time? Have you properly built yourself to this point, or is there a need to go back and pick up some elements that are missing?

2. How committed are you to lifetime learning? Can you identify a weekly time that is set aside to building yourself up as a leader?

Questions for FLOWters (Future Leaders of the World)

1. Can you identify a good mentor who can assist you in your path toward leadership development? If not, do you have a good friend who can walk the road with you?

2. What are your core values? Are they ones that you know you can build your life on in the future?

PART THREE

Application

CHAPTER TEN

Ernest Shackleton—Case Study in Ideal Leadership

Ideal Leadership ©
Case Studies Program
Ernest H. Shackleton: 1874-1922 — Antarctic Explorer Extraordinaire

PARTICIPANT'S GUIDE

Materials prepared by Larry W. Stout, Ph.D., MBA
Associate Professor of Business Psychology
Stockholm School of Economics in Riga (Latvia)

The Trans-Antarctic Expedition 1914-1917

The Endurance Expedition headed by Ernest Shackleton is one of the most extraordinary experiences of leadership on record. All aspects of Leadership Capital and the applicability of the Leadership Conditions are evidenced in this man during this event.

Ernest Shackleton

In Shackleton's own words, "After the conquest of the South Pole by Amundsen who, by a narrow margin of days only, was in advance of the British Expedition under Scott, there remained but one great main object of Antarctic journeyings—the crossing of the South Polar continent from sea to sea.

Already a celebrated polar explorer, Sir Ernest Shackleton coordinated the British Imperial Trans-Antarctic Expedition with the goal of accomplishing the first crossing of the Antarctic continent, a feat he considered to be the last great polar journey of the "Heroic Age of Exploration."

In December 1914, Shackleton set sail with his 27-man crew, many of whom, it is said, had responded to the following recruitment notice: "Men wanted for hazardous journey. Small wages. Bitter cold. Long months of complete darkness. Constant danger. Safe return doubtful. Honour and recognition in case of success. —Ernest Shackleton."

Ice conditions were unusually harsh; and the wooden ship, which Shackleton had renamed Endurance after his family motto, Fortitudine Vincimus—"by endurance we conquer"—became trapped in the pack ice of the Weddell Sea. For ten months, the Endurance drifted, locked within the ice, until the pressure crushed the ship. With meager food, clothing, and shelter, Shackleton and his men were stranded on the ice floes, where they camped for five months.

Many years after the events of the Endurance, the men were asked what kept them going during those long, dark months of despair. Their unanimous response was a single word, "Shackleton."

When they had drifted to the northern edge of the pack, encountering open leads of water, the men sailed the three small lifeboats they'd salvaged to a bleak crag called Elephant Island. They were on land for the first time in 497 days; however, it was uninhabited, and due to its distance from shipping lanes, provided no hope for rescue.

Recognizing the severity of the physical and mental strains on his men, Shackleton and five others immediately set out to take the crew's rescue into their own hands. In a 22-foot lifeboat named the James Caird, they accomplished the impossible, surviving a 17-day, 800-mile journey through the world's worst seas to South Georgia Island, where a whaling station was located.

The six men landed on an uninhabited part of the island, however, so their last hope was to cross 26 miles of mountains and glaciers, considered impassable, to reach the whaling station on the other side. Starved, frostbitten, and wearing rags, Shackleton and two others made the trek; and in August 1916, 21 months after the initial departure of the Endurance, Shackleton himself returned to rescue the men on Elephant Island. Although they'd withstood the most incredible hardship and privation, not one member of the 28-man crew was lost.

Further Study

Shackleton's adventure was largely unnoticed at the time because the events of World War I took precedence. It was not until leadership issues became much more a focus in business literature that he was suddenly "discovered." Following are several good websites that contain information on Shackleton and his expeditions:

In recent years there have been a number of special exhibitions in museums, major motion pictures, documentary films, books, magazine articles, as well as websites devoted to Shackleton and his "failed" mission. A good question to ask is WHY? What has caused the sudden interest in this particular event? Does this phenomenon illustrate the Leadership Condition of Period?

- http://www.south-pole.com/p0000098.htm   (Excellent overview on all Shackleton's explorations to the Antarctic, with good detail on the Endurance voyage in particular.)

- http://www.shackletonsantarcticadventure.com/ (Background on the IMAX film done on the Endurance Expedition. Very good resource overall, and also includes detailed information about the crew.)
- http://www.amnh.org/exhibitions/shackleton/index.html (The American Museum of National History site features diary excerpts, artifacts, and more than 150 compelling photographs by Hurley.)
- http://www.nmm.ac.uk/ (The National Maritime Museum site. Type in "Shackleton" on the search engine will direct to a good Q/A site on the man and his expedition.)
- http://wwwuk.kodak.com/US/en/corp/features/endurance/map/ (Takes a detailed look at the work of expedition photographer, Frank Hurley, with some spectacular photographs he took on the journey.)

CASE QUESTIONS

Consider Shackleton in terms of his application of Leadership Conditions (people, period, place, and position). What were they when he began the Endurance Expedition and in what ways did these increase during the crisis? In what ways did this impact his leadership effectiveness?

Consider Shackleton's Leadership Capital in each of the six competencies (vision, values, wisdom, courage, trust, voice). Which did Shackleton himself value the most? How did his Capital increase or decrease during the crisis? What impact did this have on the eventual rescue of the men?

Ideal Leadership ©
Case Studies Program
Ernest H. Shackleton: 1874-1922 — Antarctic Explorer Extraordinaire

MENTOR'S GUIDE

Materials prepared by Larry W. Stout, Ph.D., MBA,
Associate Professor of Business Psychology
Stockholm School of Economics in Riga (Latvia)

Case Analysis

Using the "Ideal Leadership" Model, evaluate the British Antarctic explorer Ernest Shackleton, particularly in relation to his leadership in the Endurance Expedition. In analyzing this case, you should consider all aspects of Leadership Capital and the applicability of the Leadership Conditions.

In Shackleton's own words, "After the conquest of the South Pole by Amundsen who, by a narrow margin of days only, was in advance of the British Expedition under Scott, there remained but one great main object of Antarctic journeyings—the crossing of the South Polar continent from sea to sea."

Ernest Shackleton's Endurance Expedition is one of the great adventure stories of all time, but it is also an excellent example of the components of leadership in action. Each of the six Leadership Capital elements are evidenced during this difficult mission.

Vision and Values

Vision was the cornerstone of the whole expedition. Though the South Pole had been discovered by Amundsen by this time, Shackleton was challenged to write the final page in Antarctica's exploration. His goal was to cross the entire Antarctic continent from sea to sea.

Though this was to be a new project, it was obviously backed by the discoveries end experiences of previous expeditions. What drove Shackleton so much in this venture was his underlying belief in the inevitability of such exploration. It would be done by him or someone later, but it definitely would someday be done!

Therefore, his vision to be part of the first expedition to cross the Antarctica was based on the following underlying ideas:

- First of all, his personal belief that it could be done—to demonstrate the ability of a man to do it. (This is what drove much of the exploration during those times.)

- Secondly, this venture would be of great historic and scientific importance.

- Finally, it would bring recognition and fame (not only for himself, but also for the whole British Empire).

Shackleton had a vision with a concrete strategy behind him, but it was united with a very strong set of values. It was the values that drove the vision, not the vision that determined the values. This was seen very vividly when the ship "Endurance" first froze in ice. The vision did not change because it was believed that the ice would break up and the journey could be completed. But when the ship was destroyed, the overriding value of safety and survival of the men took preeminence.

These values are not directly related to Shackleton's religious background, but there is certainly some evidence of that. He attached great importance to the Bible, and used his sacrifice of leaving it behind as an example to the others of the sacrifice they needed to make in their personal belongings. When Shackleton led the rescue team on the way back to Elephant Island, "...Shackleton, who was standing on the bow, to shout to Wild, 'Are you all well?' Wild replied, 'All safe, all well!' and the Boss replied, 'Thank God!'"

Wisdom and Courage

Shackleton has very well demonstrated these aspects of Leadership Capital:

- His previous expeditions to the South Pole gave him a unique experience and allowed him to gather the necessary information for the expedition.

- He understood that without money it would be impossible; therefore, he made a lot of effort to find sponsors around the world. (His cleverness in fund-raising is evidenced in that most of the public schools of England and Scotland helped the Expedition to purchase the dog teams—each dog was named after a school that contributed).

- He continually displayed wisdom in respect to his attitude towards his team. For example, he shared the day-to-day responsibilities with his crewmembers during the winter quarters in the "Ritz" or on a boat to South Georgia.

- Courage was demonstrated a number of times, the most amazing was his trip to South Georgia on a boat and a later crossing of South Georgia Island to the whaling station.

- His most important element of courage was what he himself termed as his optimism. To remain optimistic in the face of such constant dangers demanded an immense amount of courage.

Trust and Voice

These aspects of Shackleton's leadership were very certain because there was not a serious conflict between him and his team members during the expedition. As the story tells us, his decisions were not always right (for example, stopping the engines of the "Endurance" which caused it to be frozen in ice), but it never undermined the trust the men had in him.

Trust was a critical issue for Shackleton. When he was selecting his team in England, he placed *loyalty* to him as a higher value than even the particular expertise of the individual man. He knew that under the hard conditions they were about to enter, it would be absolutely imperative that his men trust him; and he chose men from the outset that he believed would do so.

His voice was an important part of his Leadership Capital. When he made a decision, it was clear and not challenged. He listened to all, but it was unmistakably clear that he was "the boss." What gave his words the most power was the fact that he himself was living by them as well. He never asked anyone to do something that he himself would not do.

Applicability of Leadership Conditions

People

Shackleton's Leadership Capital was cultivated first of all by good followers. The major factors were:

- He chose the members himself (remember, the ad in newspaper) with a certain determined attitude. Of the thousands of applicants who applied, 26 men were selected).

- He relied on his experience to work with people. For example, Frank Wild, second-in-command, accompanied Shackleton during a previous expedition; he was an executive person with no ambition to become a leader.

- He made a lot of effort to join the others (i.e. celebrations, joint games, singing, etc.).

- Also, his wisdom to choose the right people and to "hold" them was reflected in the right managing of them (e.g., to take the complainer with him to South Georgia or to place the most worrying person in command of the food stock).

Period

The period was right because it was the time of last great discoveries, and it was the time for such charismatic persons like Shackleton to do it.

The only concern was the beginning of World War I. (Shackleton offered the ship and the services to the country, but he was commanded to "proceed.")

Place

His culture and career (sailing and participation in expeditions) in Britain at that time fit perfectly with his personality. He was a visionary who loved exploration, but at the same time, was a "detail" man who took every precaution of safety.

Position

Position of the leader as well as his title in the British Empire at that time determined his authority as a leader. He was called the "Boss" by his men because his position was unquestioned.

It can truly be said that Ernest Shackleton was the right man, serving at the right time, doing the right things, for the right people, which enabled him to serve in a leadership capacity. Because his Leadership Capital was so high, he was able to succeed in an "impossible mission" where so many others would have failed.

CHAPTER ELEVEN

Ideal Leadership Development Plan (ILDP) Workbook

Ideal Leadership ©
ILDP Program
Ideal Leadership Development Plan (ILDP) Workbook

PARTICIPANT'S GUIDE

Materials prepared by Larry W. Stout, Ph.D., MBA
Associate Professor of Business Psychology
Stockholm School of Economics in Riga (Latvia)

Personal Leadership Development

Everyone should have a desire for lifelong learning, but it is best when these energies can be directed toward goals that will provide worthwhile benefits. The following exercises are designed to assist in discovering a path for personal leadership development.

Do not rush through these exercises. Answer them and then put your answers away and look at them later. The more honest you are, the better you will be able to truly reflect on your own leadership development.

The first step in developing a personal development plan in leadership is to conduct an assessment of your present Leadership Capital. If you do not have the opportunity to take the Ideal Leadership Capital Assessment©, then answer the following questions and discuss them with a mentor or fellow traveler in leadership to establish where your strengths and weaknesses currently lie.

Vision

- Do you have a real dream? (If so, answer this question: "What magazine cover would you like to be on some day and for what reason?")

- Before you make key decisions in your life, do you first analyze how they will impact your life's dream?

- Do you have an inner drive that comes from an innate feeling that you are destined to accomplish something important?

Values

- Do you deal with problems and crises from a situational or a moral base? (Try to think of specific examples.)

- Do those around you sense a certain value standard that you will not break?

- Who do you look up to the most? What characteristic does he or she possess that you most admire?

Wisdom

- Do you recognize your weaknesses? Are you able to practice good self-awareness?

- What are you reading? Are you continually seeking to increase your personal and professional knowledge?

- Do you critically examine information? Do you try to go beyond what is expected and develop something different and better?

Courage

- In everyday life, are you willing to take risks? In what circumstances? How do you evaluate risk?

- Do you give up or look for excuses during difficult projects? Do you continue to search for alternatives? Do you like to be flexible and play hunches?

- Does your decision-making show creativity, intuition and insight, or rely mostly on tried and true methods?

If you are currently not leading others, the Trust and Voice questions are sometimes difficult to answer. Think of some circumstances, perhaps even in voluntary organizations or even in family roles, when you were responsible for others.

Trust

- Do you blame others for your career path or difficulties?

- How many people can you name, who would act on your word without question (not in a directive sense, but in a desirable sense)?

- Do you know individuals on whom you can place areas of your own personal responsibility? In other words, how do you practice delegation?

Voice

- What key idea, principle, or concept do you hold with absolute conviction?

- What influence do you have over others when communicating with them? How well are you able to maintain "control" over those subordinate to you?

- Think of one or two words that others would use to describe you. Would these word(s) change depending on who would be asked?

Next Step

The case study example of Ernest Shackleton shows that key events can be quickly summarized in a biographical sketch. Imagine if your life was going to be used for a case study. How would you describe your life story in 400-500 words?

- These life highlights do not have to be the best events; they can also be failures.

- Seek to identify the key factors behind these life highlights. In other words, not just "what" happened, but "why."

- If you had to give a title to this story, what would it be? Try to think of a metaphor (race, battle, song, etc.) that would best sum up your life to this point.

PUTTING TOGETHER YOUR "CASE"

Try to track your life story along an x/y axis, with the horizonal line representing time and the vertical line representing maturity or growth. The highlight events mark turning points; they represent either GOLI's or FOLI's. Review these demarcation points to determine any pattern. Write your reflections in a few sentences.

Now match your reflections with your answers to the six competencies. In what areas did you have the greatest difficulty in answering? Do you see any correlation to the GOLI/FOLI points in your life chart?

Using this exercise, pinpoint one or two key areas you believe would best help you develop in the future. For example, perhaps you notice that you have had a series of FOLI's in your life that seem to stem from poor decision-making skills, and you find that the questions in the Wisdom area were the most difficult for you to answer. This would seem to indicate that Wisdom is an important area for you to focus on in the future.

Ideal Leadership ©
ILDP Program
Ideal Leadership Development Plan (ILDP) Workbook

MENTOR'S GUIDE

Materials prepared by Larry W. Stout, Ph.D., MBA
Associate Professor of Business Psychology
Stockholm School of Economics in Riga (Latvia)

Designing an ILDP

A good coach or mentor should try to assist the individual in making personal self-discoveries—not giving them answers. We learn best what we learn ourselves. Through the exercises, try to listen to the answers behind the answers. Help the individual understand themselves.

> *The questions offered here are meant to be catalysts to discussion. The main idea is to get the individual to honestly reflect on his or her competence in each of the six Leadership Capital areas.*

The questions in the Participants Guide under each competency are designed to probe deep into the individual. There is a danger that he or she will answer what the coach or mentor wants to hear. If this happens, the following are additional questions that could help confront the individual into answering honestly.

Vision

- What book has had the most profound influence on your life? (If the individual cannot name a book, ask him to name a film, or anything, that has had a role in shaping his thinking. Our vision is often formed by the challenges we gain from others.)

- Name one person, alive or dead, whom you would most like to meet and talk to, for one hour. (If the individual has a real dream, he will want to talk with someone who he believes can give him insight on how to make the dream come to life. The one-hour deadline helps him think about discussing the most critical issues with this person.)

Values

- For one million dollars, would you be willing to (1) kill your neighbor's favorite pet? (2) deny your friend an important promotion? (3) keep a discovery secret that could potentially save money for thousands of poor people? (4) spend a year in prison? (These questions, and any others you can think of, help the person understand how strong his personal convictions really are.)

- If your house or apartment was on fire and you had time to grab only one thing (not a person, they will escape without your help), what object would you want to take and why? (This helps identify what is most important. It might be money, or a picture, or a particular book or diary. Why is this so important to him or her? What does it represent?)

- More than anything else, what is the one thing in life that you want to prevent from happening? (The answer helps to clarify the individual's values. The thing they do not want to happen is something that they are willing to work hardest toward.)

Wisdom

- If you could "Google" God, what would you ask? (The depth of the question shows the depth of their critical thinking.)

- What motto or saying do you want to appear on your tombstone? (Though this is a somewhat morbid thought, it causes people to think about the totality of life and how they want to summarize the culmination of their life.)

Life Metaphors and Values: Ask the individual to complete the statement—"Life is a _____." The metaphor chosen speaks about their life values. For example: Life is a race (speed), battle (victory or struggle), game (challenge), song (joy), puzzle (solutions or answers)

Courage

- If you were given $1,000 USD and had a chance to either keep it or wager it all for a ten-percent chance at $10,000, which would you choose? (Though it is easy to risk when the case is imaginary, try to pin the person down to think about it realistically. The vast majority of people select the sure $1,000 over the ten-percent chance for ten times that amount.)

- Kurt Wallenda said that when he was on the high wire (without a net), he was truly "alive." What do you do in life that makes you come alive? (These are generally events in life that involve some creativity or risk. Are they in personal areas or professional ones?)

Trust

- How would you describe a friend? (The qualities chosen often describe what aspects of trust are most valued.)

- What is the biggest trust "buster" for you? (Again, the answer reveals much about what aspect of trust is most highly valued.)

Voice

- Think of three words that best describe your life. Now stand in front of someone and deliver these three words in a 30-second time frame. (Obviously a person does not need 30 seconds to say three words. However, what they should do is attempt to thrust as much intensity into each word as possible. Can they communicate the depth of importance in each of these words by their presence and voice?)

- What types of people seem to listen to you the best? Why do you believe this is true? (This question helps the individual know what types make up their Leadership Condition of "people.")

Life Story Exercise

After the individual writes a 400-500 word review of his life, help him identify his own GOLI's and FOLI's—try making an analogy to a game.

- If your life were a game, what would be the objective of the game? In other words, how would you win?

- If you know how you would win, how would you be keeping score? In other words, what measurement are you using to determine successes (GOLI's) and failures (FOLI's)?

- What are the rules of your game? Where are the boundaries? What would constitute a foul? (This last question is very important in helping to bring into focus the philosophical competency areas.)

Developing an ILDP

The objective of all these exercises is to pinpoint in what priority should focus be given to build Leadership Capital.

If **vision** is needed, study cases of great visionary leaders. Try to pinpoint where their vision came from. Seek to draw out from the individual what he believes his life is best designed to accomplish.

If **values** are needed, complete the exercises that help clarify what values the individual most needs to accomplish the vision he desires. These values also need to be grounded beyond the individual himself—spiritual foundations are the best answer.

If **wisdom** is needed, the individual needs to become self-aware that he needs to work at becoming a better problem-solver and decision-maker. More than anything else, encourage the individual to continue his professional reading.

If **courage** is needed, make the individual aware of his caution and the reasons behind it. He needs to take steps forward—and build his confidence.

If **trust** is needed, help the individual to practice better interpersonal skills, especially listening. Is he putting deposits into the "trust bank" of others? If not, why not?

If **voice** is needed, guide the individual into recognizing his own key voice distinction, and find the best ways to articulate this in all he does. This will help him build confidence and grow.

Each of these should have tangible goals with difficult-to-reach targets that can be measured over a given period of time. Once one goal is reached, establish the next one, and so forth, for a lifetime process of personal leadership development.

Ideal Leadership Series

BOOK 1
Ideal Leadership: Time for a Change

This book introduces the Ideal Leadership Model and its implementation through the seven leadership essentials that describe the nature of leadership and why some succeed and others fail.

BOOK 2
Ideal Leadership: Capital Gain or Pain

This book elaborates on the Ideal Leadership Model, specifically focusing on the six Leadership Capital competencies of vision, values, trust, voice, wisdom, and courage.

BOOK 3
Ideal Leadership: Moving Up and Moving Out

This book discusses the four conditions necessary for a leader to be able to initiate change within an organization: period (time), place (domain), position (authority), and people (followers), and how a leader can develop his or her Leadership Conditions more strategically.

Book 4
Ideal Leadership: Good GOLI's!

This book examines the Gateways of Leadership Initiative (GOLI's), the leadership moments that move an organization forward, contrasted with the Failures of Leadership Initiative (FOLI's) that ultimately bring an organization down.

Book 5
Ideal Leadership: Success on Seven Continents

This book relates true-life stories where Ideal Leadership has been implemented in business, government, nonprofit organizations, and religious organizations around the world.

CONTACT THE AUTHOR

Those interested in contacting Dr. Stout or learning more about leadership development based on the Ideal Leadership Model should visit the website:

www.idealleadership.com.